Encounters
with
Teaching

a
Microteaching Manual

THOMAS B. GREGORY
Indiana University

Prentice-Hall, Inc., Englewood Cliffs, New Jersey

© 1972 by Prentice-Hall, Inc., Englewood Cliffs, New Jersey

ISBN: 0-13-274936-X

Library of Congress Catalog Card Number: 76-38891

Printed in the United States of America

Current Printing:

10   9   8   7   6   5   4   3   2   1

74 - 2384

Prentice-Hall International, Inc., London
Prentice-Hall of Australia, Pty. Ltd., Sydney
Prentice-Hall of Canada, Ltd., Toronto
Prentice-Hall of India Private Limited, New Delhi
Prentice-Hall of Japan, Inc., Tokyo

To O. L. and the Texas Gang
and
the F100 Crew,
my two sojourns on Rabbit Mountain

Contents

1

Microteaching Concerns
1

vii

2
Process Concerns
21

3
Affective Concerns
81

4

Personal Concerns

127

Preface

The focus of this microteaching manual was shaped by the confluence of several forces which are dramatically reshaping the direction of education today. One is represented in education's post-Sputnik concern with process. Since Bruner's now classic thesis that "any subject can be taught effectively in some intellectually honest form to any child at any stage of development" (1960), the profession has witnessed the development, refinement, dissemination, and assimilation of numerous curriculum projects, all incorporating process as content to help students think like scientists, mathematicians, anthropologists, or whatever.

Another force centers on education's increasing attention to the affect (feeling) in the classroom. More and more teachers are coming to feel the squeeze of the "content press" that has defined many personal concerns of teachers and students as illegitimate subject matter. We live in our gut and we react on the basis of our feelings, but we raise generations of children who are so inexperienced at consciously dealing with feelings that their most rudimentary attempts at communicating them often fail miserably.

A third force manifests itself in teacher education's expanding attempts to bring the reality of the public school classroom onto the college campus via microteaching and other simulated classroom experiences. Such teaching laboratory activities are rapidly breaking down the traditional and largely fallacious dichotomy of theory and practice by providing concomitant, concrete teaching experiences to which the abstractions of the college classroom may be applied.

Yet another force is the concept embodied in a growing pool of research (Fuller, 1969) suggesting that traditional teacher preparation programs do little to meet the personal concerns of their increasingly frustrated and alienated clientele. These studies indicate that in the pre-teaching phase of his professional training, the beginning teacher's concerns are highly personal and may have little to do with teaching (non-concern). Teaching laboratory experience quickly moves him into the early teaching phase (concern with self) and provides a supportive, low-risk environment in which he can begin reconciling this group of concerns. Subsequent course work can then focus on his later concerns (concern with students). This last phase would include seeking answers to questions such as "What is it about the school as a social institution that impedes or facilitates teaching and learning?", and "Why are schools the way they are?"

Students have long directed criticism at the courses encountered early in their teacher preparation program. Much of their commentary begins to make sense if one notes that the foundations-related content of such courses is generally of most concern to experienced, not inexperienced teachers. The continuum of concerns, in fact, suggests that teacher preparation is essentially built upside-down with personal experience coming *last* and objective examination of the larger educational ethic coming *first*. Student teaching should not occur early in the program, but research indicates that some sort of personal, quasi-realistic encounters with teaching should be experienced as soon as possible. The teaching laboratory may not be a cure for this particular curricular disease, but by treating the symptoms, it has proven its ability to at least reduce the patient's pain.

All these forces are of crucial importance and this manual attempts to utilize the productive energy implicit in each of them. It attempts to teach the beginning teacher a set of process and affective skills that will enable him to easily adapt to the new curricula he will hopefully encounter. A related objective of this manual, and perhaps its prime one, is to provide a set of activities through which a beginning teacher can have an early encounter with himself as a teacher. The information gained from that experience will hopefully help him make significant strides toward arriving at an early, knowledgeable decision about a teaching career. To purport that this small manual can fully accomplish these grandiose objectives is indeed naive. It simply points beginning teachers in the direction of the respective paths of these objectives through a series of *Encounters with Teaching.*

Acknowledgments

Many people helped write this book. O. L. Davis, Jr. of The University of Texas at Austin, Ronald T. Hyman of Rutgers University, and David Young of The University of Maryland provided many helpful suggestions which resulted in a significant reconstruction of the original manuscript, particularly Parts I and II.

Robert R. Carkhuff of American International College and my colleagues, Marcia Buchanan, Keith M. Miser, and John L. Werner gave many helpful comments on Part III. The latter two also aided considerably in the field testing of the affective tasks presented in that part of the manual.

Robert Brashear of Western Michigan University, Paul Kirby of the Southwest Regional Laboratory, and Marcy Kysilka of Florida Technical University donated both their class time and students to perform a field test of a preliminary version of Parts I, II, and IV.

Chriss Scott and my wife, Diane, edited various drafts of the manuscript.

Mary Ann Abel, Donna Bailey, and Trisa Van Sell all tackled the herculean task of deciphering my atrocious handwriting and typing the various drafts of the manuscript.

Many others could also be mentioned, if for no other reason than for the many ways in which their ideas have influenced my thinking. I trust they will understand their omission as nothing more than an author's quest for brevity.

Using This Manual
A Note to the Teaching Laboratory Instructor

The ordering of tasks presented in this manual is only one of several that make sense. Moreover, few microteaching settings will encourage the use of all nine tasks. The format of the manual allows alternatives.

Suggestions for Reordering Tasks

A good argument can be presented for considering the affective tasks as representing a set of basic teaching strategies which should be mastered *before* attempting the process tasks. Reorderings of the affective tasks are also easily accomplished.

The ordering of the process tasks is less easily changed but the following procedure is not without merit. First, the teacher attempts to teach a long microlesson incorporating the entire problem-solving act (Tasks Two through Four) but is evaluated only on how well he fulfills Task Four's objectives. Second, he reteaches the microlesson but is now evaluated on how well he fulfills both Task Four and Task Three's objectives.

Finally, he again reteaches the microlesson but is now evaluated on how well he fulfills the objectives of all three process tasks.

Yet another reordering might intersperse the affective tasks among the process tasks so that the teacher masters both affective and process teaching strategies simultaneously. Here the teach phase (see p. 5) of an appropriate affective task could be introduced in the reteach phase of a process task and, in turn, the teach phase of the next process task could be introduced in the reteach phase of the previous affective task and so on. Note, however, that the complexity of such a condensation makes mastery of teaching strategies extremely demanding for the teacher.

Suggestions for Eliminating Tasks

If one counts the reteach phases for Tasks Two through Eight, a teacher using this entire manual will teach sixteen microlessons. This represents an extensive microteaching experience. Most situations will call for considerably fewer microlessons, and some tasks will therefore be dropped. There are several ways of doing this.

Task One may not be required if the teacher has already had a previous microteaching experience. Accordingly, Task Nine may be dropped if the teacher will be moving immediately into more microteaching activities.

A methods course context may suggest concentrating on the process section and foregoing the affective tasks, while a general introductory course containing teachers of many different subjects may call for the reverse situation. Other situations may warrant using some tasks of each type. For example, Task Three which deals with hypothesizing and Task Eight ("Communicating Concretely") may be much more important in a science context than in a drama context. Here Task Four, which includes introspecting and several of the affective tasks, may seem more appropriate. In other situations, some of the affective tasks may be eliminated or combined.

Perhaps the most interesting approach might be to allow each teacher to pick whatever number of tasks he sees as most valuable for him. He could also determine the order in which he would work on them.

Your situation should dictate the format you decide to use. One of microteaching's prime attractions is its flexibility. Try to capitalize on it.

*Encounters
with
Teaching*

1

Microteaching Concerns

1

Microteaching and the Teaching Laboratory

Most teacher education programs contain three basic components: course work, observations in the schools, and student teaching. The rationale for such a program is fairly obvious. Courses attempt to give you the prerequisite knowledge of facts and principles necessary for teaching; observations allow you to relate this knowledge to real situations; and student teaching permits you to gain experience in applying your newly acquired professional knowledge and allows you to further develop your teaching skills. This model has been widely accepted.

Such a traditional program is insufficient because it defines much of your preparation for teaching as passive instead of active, unrealistic instead of realistic, and general instead of specific. At least one additional phase is desirable, one consisting of a series of laboratory components. These components, which include microteaching and other methods of simulating teaching situations, have been collectively referred to as the teaching laboratory.

The Teaching Laboratory

The teaching laboratory's purpose is to bring more activity, reality, and specificity to phases of teacher preparation prior to student teaching (Broudy, 1964; Davis and Gregory, 1968, 1970). Think of a continuum such as that represented in Figure 1.

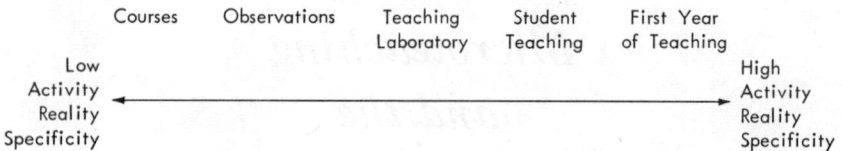

	Courses	Observations	Teaching Laboratory	Student Teaching	First Year of Teaching	
Low Activity Reality Specificity			⟵————————————————⟶			High Activity Reality Specificity

The teaching laboratory is an environment for encouraging the early relation and application of knowledge, and the development of skills. It also acts as an intermediate agent that enhances the probabilities of transfer of knowledge and skills learned in the college classroom to the public school classroom by reducing the perceived dissimilarities of the two settings. The teaching laboratory has also functioned effectively in in-service settings by helping experienced teachers improve their teaching.

The teaching laboratory is a small room equipped with the basic classroom furnishings, including desks, a blackboard, an overhead projector, and easy access to other standard instructional aids. It also contains audiovisual equipment to record the activities of teachers. These records provide accurate and realistic feedback to the teacher using the laboratory.

The teaching laboratory also contains from four to eight "students" who may be real students recruited from the public schools or other teachers role-playing students of a given age and ability level. The latter source of "students," with its lower reality level, has proven to be an expedient but less desirable alternative, especially for a teacher's early experience in the teaching laboratory.

Microteaching

During the summer of 1963, the Secondary Teacher Education Program at Stanford University launched a new laboratory experience in the pre-service preparation of its teaching interns. The idea upon which the new program was based was simple: give interns pre-service teaching experience in a highly structured laboratory setting where risk of failure was low and opportunities for refining teaching skills were high. Because this setting was to be a scaled-down encounter with teaching, the lessons were kept short (five to twenty minutes), the number of students was kept small (one to five), and the instructional task for a lesson was well defined. The new laboratory experience was called, appropriately, "microteaching."

"Fundamentally, microteaching is an idea, at the core of which lie five essential propositions: . . ." Microteaching is *real teaching* [1] that *lessens the complexities* of normal classroom teaching for you by *focusing on training* you to accomplish specific tasks, thus allowing for *increased control* of your practice which, in turn, gives a *focus to your feedback* that allows it to be greatly expanded beyond the usual knowledge-of-results dimension you would normally experience in teaching (Allen and Ryan, 1969, pp. 2–3).

While microteaching you are required, among other tasks, to incorporate specific teaching strategies into short lessons (microlessons) ranging from five to twenty minutes in length. When not teaching, you may be acting as a student for another teacher. In all cases, you are an observer and describer/evaluator, providing feedback through written and spoken comments on microlessons taught by your colleagues and yourself.

In this manual, several related teaching strategies are grouped together in each "task" or microteaching assignment. Communicating how to use these teaching strategies is often quite difficult and might be likened to the inefficiency of attempting to describe, through words alone, how to perform some physical act (e.g., *showing* someone how to serve a volleyball is much more instructive than *telling* him how). To facilitate communication of the exact nature of these complex tasks, microteaching is often designed as a trial and error situation called a teach-reteach cycle. The cycle improves communication by giving a teacher two opportunities not only to understand the nature of the task, but also to assimilate the strategies of which it is comprised. The teach-reteach cycle includes six steps:

Teach Phase

1. Prepare a microlesson incorporating the requirements of the assigned task.
2. Teach your microlesson.
3. Receive oral, written, and recorded feedback on how well you have accomplished your teaching task.

Reteach Phase

4. Reorganize your microlesson in light of this feedback.
5. Reteach your microlesson.
6. Again receive oral, written, and recorded feedback that, in this case, focuses on the improvements that you have or have not made.

[1] The amount of realism in microteaching is debatable; it certainly varies from situation to situation. This manual views microteaching as a *simulation* of real teaching.

The reteach phase of the cycle is sometimes optional. Some less complicated tasks do not require it (e.g., Task One: Introductory Microlesson; see Chapter 2). Occasionally the teach phase will go so well that you and/or your teaching laboratory instructor may decide the reteach phase is unnecessary. The reteach phase is always valuable when it can be taught to a new group of students that may well respond to the microlesson in a very different manner from the teach phase group.

Microteaching adapts to a wide variety of situations. The diversity of procedural models possible may be illustrated by the following three examples. A program is not likely to follow any one of the three exactly, nor should it. Rather, a program should dictate a model that best satisfies its own unique requirements and constraints.[2] You need read only those model descriptions assigned by your laboratory instructor. If he assigned none of them, skip to the description of this manual on page 9.

Clinic model. The clinic model operates independently of any course. This approach uses real students who may even receive remuneration for their work, and it must, therefore, have a schedule that does not conflict with the public schools. As a result, clinic approaches are often conducted during the summer months. Several teaching laboratories are established to allow equipment, staff, and hired students to be used efficiently. A teacher works on tasks individually with a supervisor. A group of students is brought into the room. The teacher teaches a microlesson (teach phase) which is either audio or video tape recorded. At its conclusion, the students give the teacher a written and/or oral evaluation of his teaching and then leave. The teacher then has a private conference with his supervisor. Strengths and weaknesses are reviewed and pertinent segments of the recording are heard/viewed. The teacher then again prepares his microlesson, eliminating its weak points, and reteaches it to a different group of students. The new students evaluate the microlesson and leave. The teacher then has a second brief conference with his supervisor.

The entire procedure takes about an hour, making it the most efficient model in terms of the teacher time required. Since the teacher does not also have to role-play a student for some of his colleagues (see next two models), he is only responsible for his own teaching.

Operation of a clinic approach to microteaching can be an expensive undertaking. The logistics and financing required for equipment, supporting staff, supervisor, and students are formidable indeed. The clinic model has many advantages: it intensifies learning; it maximizes reality

---

[2] See Allen and Ryan (1969) for additional information about various adaptations of microteaching.

and the immediacy of feedback; tasks can readily be individually prescribed; and much individual attention is provided. Something resembling the clinic model, what might be called *macro*teaching, works well in student teaching and in-service applications. Here, the students taught are the teacher's normal class, and the length of the lesson expands to the normal school period, consequently rendering the prefix "micro" meaningless.

Intra-course model. Microteaching can also be adapted to an existing course in the teacher preparation sequence. In such a context, it provides a group of prospective teachers with a common set of concrete teaching experiences to which the abstract content of the course (including theory) can be related. Though most often associated with a methods course, microteaching can function in a broad variety of settings. In the introductory course, it provides a person with concrete, personal data about himself as a teacher that can be valuable in making a career choice. In the educational psychology course, microteaching can focus on learning problems and aspects of human relations. Applications of microteaching have merit even in history and philosophy courses. "The behaviors a [teacher] exhibits while teaching, eloquently herald his real philosophy of education, his logic and ethics, far more than the most cogently manicured paragraph of a term paper or panel discussion" (Davis and Gregory, 1970, p. 204).

The intra-course model requires that at least one day of class each week be set aside for microteaching. The class is divided up into laboratory groups small enough to permit all the members of each group to teach their microlesson and receive feedback within the scheduled time period. Since all groups teach simultaneously, a separate teaching laboratory is needed for each. Members of the group role-play students and evaluate microlessons for each other. The instructor moves from group to group as much as possible to provide additional supervisory help, but each group is trained to be a fairly autonomous unit operating its own equipment and drawing upon its own members for ideas, advice, criticism, and support. Group membership is stable, changing only when the members feel a need for "fresh blood." The tape recordings of microlessons are available for individual hearing/viewing during the ensuing week. A portion of a second class day each week is devoted to problems encountered in the last microlesson and those anticipated in the next assigned task.

While the intra-course model considerably reduces the amount of trained supervisory feedback and the realism afforded by the clinic model, it contains several distinct advantages. The intra-course model can be used effectively even with very large numbers of students. It can operate, with some strain, even within a forty-five to sixty-minute time block if the number of teaching laboratories is sufficient to allow laboratory groups to be small enough to permit members to finish their work in the allotted time. Teachers have sufficient planning time between the teach and reteach phases to prepare an entirely new microlesson if necessary. As previously stated, microteaching also provides the class members with a common concrete experience to which they can relate the abstractions presented in the course. Small group work also promotes class cohesiveness and facilitates the cross-fertilization of ideas.

Extra-course model.   The time constraints of the intra-course model can be appreciably reduced by making microteaching activities an adjunct to an existing course, something that might be termed a "mini-course." Here microteaching functions as one of several elective or required experiences. Released time may be given from a specific course for microteaching activities or the microteaching experience may, in effect, be a separate course. Small groups of teachers work together much as they do in intra-class applications. The main difference is that members may come from various sections of one course or various different courses and the structure of the experience dictates the schedule followed. This situation is thus the opposite of the one arising in intra-course applications. The extra-course model sufficiently extends the meeting time to permit all members to complete the entire teach-reteach cycle, rather than only half of it. The model may use real students for a part or all of the microteaching experience if the schedule and facilities of a nearby public school permit the use of volunteer students from study halls. The extra-course model contains advantages of both the clinic and intra-class models. It is essentially a combination of the two because of the opportunities it affords for group learning while requiring minimal scheduling restrictions.

Modeling.   The effectiveness of each of the foregoing approaches can be enhanced by providing ideal examples or models of the kind of teaching being asked for in a specific task. The models can be presented via typescripts, audio or video tape recordings, or films. Research indicates that models can be so influential that a teacher's behavior can be changed simply by observing the behavior of others and the consequences of that behavior. The observing teacher need not actually perform the behavior himself (Bandura and Walters, 1963; Koran, 1969).

The effectiveness of modeling has led many to devise microteaching approaches that take advantage of its power to alter teaching behavior.

One such approach attempts to maximize changes in teaching behavior in situations having very high teacher/laboratory instructor ratios.[3]

Basically, this approach has the instructor model the desired teaching strategies for a group of teachers by teaching and recording an appropriate microlesson. The recording is then played back to the group with the instructor providing cues to focus the teachers' attention on the strategies involved in the task.

This exercise has several advantages. It aids the development of the teachers' ability to identify the desired behaviors, thus improving the quality of the feedback they will give each other. By attempting (probably imperfectly) the task first, the laboratory instructor helps his teachers identify the realistic constraints of that microlesson. Seeing the "expert" have problems can promote a relaxed atmosphere where mistakes are not failures but stimuli to learning.

After the modeling activity, the instructor working with a large group of teachers can divide them into small groups in which the members teach their microlessons to each other. The instructor moves from group to group, observing, assisting, and providing support and additional feedback.

Later, the groups can be brought back together to view and respond to randomly selected microlessons. Each teacher can, at some later time, view his own microlesson and personally critique it. Such a procedure also reduces the social pressure on those teachers who are experiencing high levels of ego-involvement (see p. 12).

The Manual

This manual is designed to introduce you to some of the important teaching strategies identified by educational and psychological research. Teaching is, in part, a psychomotor task in much the same sense that driving, acting, typing, and playing a musical instrument are. Obviously, learning any of these activities involves acquiring the necessary cognitive skills. But in addition, none of these tasks can be adequately learned without mastering their physical requirements. Mastery of this kind is generally best accomplished through actual practice of the actual skill or a closely related physical activity. This manual's purpose is to help you experiment with widely accepted teaching behaviors by practicing them in a situation closely resembling that found in a real classroom but void of many of a real classroom's concomitant risks (e.g., possible loss of

[3] My friend and colleague, John L. Werner, developed the specific modeling procedure described here.

student respect). The teaching laboratory's low-risk environment elimi-
nates the fight-for-survival syndrome and thereby permits you to experiment with new teaching styles and to work on improving your teaching
behavior. Microteaching also provides you with a set of real, personal
teaching experiences that will challenge or reinforce many of your conscious and unconscious attitudes and values about teaching. One of
microteaching's very real, though almost totally undocumented characteristics is its power to change attitudes. The self-knowledge gained
through its system of feedback also has the power to alter your attitudes
about yourself as a teacher. If you are still trying to make a career choice,
your teaching laboratory experience will therefore become valuable data
for you to use in attempting to answer the ultimate question: *Should
you teach?*

2

TASK ONE
What Kind of Teacher Am I?
Introductory Microlesson

The requirements for this first microlesson are quite simple. You are to teach a short lesson eight minutes in length on some curriculum-relevant topic in the teaching laboratory.[1]

One purpose of this task is to give you an opportunity to confront yourself as a teacher, perhaps for the first time. Unconsciously, you have been becoming a teacher for a long time. You have been taught many things by many people over many years. A natural byproduct of being taught is learning not only *what* is intentionally being taught (the content), but also *how* you are being taught (the process). Since you have already learned much, both good and bad, about the process of teaching, you are a kind of teacher right now. This microlesson gives you an opportunity to begin seeking an answer to the question, "What kind of teacher am I?"

Besides getting used to yourself as a teacher, you also can begin getting used to the teaching laboratory. Just as jumping into the water is a

---

[1] Individual situations may call for very different time periods ranging from four or five minutes up to much longer lessons.

prerequisite to learning how to swim, getting some first hand experience in the teaching laboratory is a prerequisite to learning and effectively applying specific strategies in later microlessons. Being anxious or nervous during this first microlesson is not atypical. You should be concerned if you are not nervous; small amounts of anxiety can be quite helpful in motivating you to perform your teaching tasks more effectively. There are at least three characteristics of this first microlesson that may contribute to your nervousness, and one purpose of this task is to give you an opportunity to overcome them.

First, it is not unusual for you to be concerned about many matters of great personal importance. Some examples are what to do with your hands, how to move about the room in a casual manner, how to anticipate your students' reaction to your microlesson, and how to avoid any undesirable speech mannerisms you might have. Such concerns disappear with experience, but they can be disconcerting to the beginner. Recognition of this point should help you reduce any anxiety associated with such matters. This introductory microlesson also gives you an opportunity to reconcile some of the cosmetic concerns that often accompany video taping so that they will not interfere with the task orientation of your ensuing microlessons.

Second, teaching in general and especially microteaching can be termed an ego-involvement situation (Sherif and Cantril, 1947). You probably come to teaching with a well-established conception of yourself and your own personal competencies. For instance, you would not be here if you did not think you could be a good teacher. In microteaching, you are confronted with the necessity to "prove" to yourself that your assessment of your own competence is correct. You are, in other words, ego-involved. This first microlesson gives you an opportunity to begin receiving meaningful feedback to use in assessing how realistic your self-concept is regarding your ability as a teacher.

Third, any time you perform (in a behavioral rather than a theatrical sense), you are unconsciously aware that you are being evaluated. For example, think of the number of unsolicited clarifying statements (giving examples, paraphrasing, asking for agreement, interjecting qualifying statements) you make in everyday conversation to insure that others will accurately understand your position. You will become very conscious of this normally unconscious behavior in microteaching since your performance is being *formally* evaluated. The problem is compounded by the additional awareness that part of that evaluation may be made by your peers. Since everyone places high value on peer status, any threat to it is anxiety-producing. Since this microlesson is not formally evaluated it gives you an opportunity to begin coping with whatever anxieties you may have. You also have the opportunity to make some important first steps in terms of a *self*-evaluation of your teaching behavior.

Some beginning teachers feel that they "just have to teach," that no other course is open to them, that not to teach would be a great personal failure. The anxiety produced by the thought of failure results in a very high level of motivation—in some cases, too high. For some, anxiety is so great that it impairs performance and must be reduced to facilitate optimal performance in the teaching laboratory. If you find yourself in this position, a consultation with your instructor may produce the means for solving your individual problem.

The Teaching Task

To repeat, your task is to prepare and teach an eight-minute microlesson in your subject area. Your only requirement is that it be curriculum relevant; choose a topic that would legitimately be taught in a public school classroom. At first, you may feel that eight minutes is not enough time to adequately teach anything. This is not the case. Most long lessons are really made up of many short segments connected by transitions. Roughly plan in outline form a fifty-minute lesson by setting down the procedure you might follow. Examine each of the major outline headings and you will find that most can be treated in eight minutes or less. Select anyone of these as the topic of your first microlesson. It can be the beginning, middle, or end of the larger lesson. By analogy, you are being asked to think of a theme topic for a term paper, but are required to prepare only one paragraph of the total project.

In microteaching, you may encounter a "clean slate" problem—the largely fallacious idea that you must always teach everyone and everything from the beginning. An examination of several textbooks in just one area of your teaching field will produce vast differences in the ordering of topics. Such an exercise reveals that each field has many possible starting points for instruction. Nevertheless, some topics do require certain prerequisite knowledge. If your microlesson topic requires such knowledge, the necessary information can be "taught" by giving your students a prepared handout containing the necessary information. Admittedly, some topics are inappropriate for the teaching laboratory, but they are far fewer than you might imagine.

The time limit is not crucial. Your microlesson can be as short as four or five minutes if you like. You may find it helpful to receive a signal after five or six minutes so that you can smoothly bring your microlesson to a close. Assume that at eight minutes the bell has rung, and your students will have to leave for their next class and you must conclude your lesson as quickly as possible.

Checking Overall Learning

This is your first of several microteaching activities. These activities are designed to help you examine and alter your teaching behavior and attitudes about teaching. The last task in this manual (Chapter 16) gives you an opportunity to assess just how much behavior and attitude change has taken place during your teaching laboratory work. That assessment can be enhanced considerably if the recording of this first microlesson can be preserved for comparison with your culminating microlesson. Magnetic tape will yield a far more accurate record of the teacher you are now than will your most vivid reconstructions from memory.

Task Objectives

So that you will better understand the criteria used to assess each microlesson, they are stated in behavioral terms (see p. 17). Since this first task has very little structure and involves little formal evaluation, it does not require the several instructional objectives necessary for subsequent, more structured tasks.[2]

Task One Objectives

1. You should be able to teach an eight minute lesson segment on some curriculum-relevant topic.

Task One Viewing/Listening Guide [3]

Name _____

This guide is designed to assist you in structuring your tape viewing/listening so that this feedback component of the teaching laboratory will be of maximum benefit to you. Please complete and return it to your instructor before you teach your next microlesson.

---

[2] Nor does this task require a formal evaluation guide as will subsequent tasks.
[3] This form may be reproduced in limited quantities without prior permission for nonprofit instructional purposes.

1. What were your dominant feelings and impressions as you taught this first micro-lesson? Of what were you most aware?

   _____

   _____

   _____

2. To what do you attribute these feelings and impressions?

   _____

   _____

3. As you view (or listen to) your tape recording, what aspects of it are most important to you? Why?

   _____

   _____

   _____

   _____

4. What were you most concerned about during the microteaching? Did you worry more about how well your students were learning or how well you were teaching?

   _____

   _____

   _____

5. Did any aspects of your lesson go better than you expected them to? Why?

   _____

   _____

6. Did any aspects of your lesson fail to meet your expectations? Why?

   _____

   _____

   _____

   _____

7. What are you saying a teacher is by the manner in which you taught this micro-lesson?

   _____

   _____

   _____

In terms of the above information, identify those aspects of your teaching that you see a need to improve. How do you intend to attack these problems? How would you have taught this microlesson differently if this had been a "real" teaching situation? Write your comments on a separate page.

3

Providing Feedback
on Teaching

One of a teacher's most difficult and important tasks is making fair, accurate evaluations (feedback) of his students' performances. The difficulty of the task is compounded when evaluation must be accompanied by grading. Any time one is asked to describe everything he knows about another human being by a letter or numeral, he tries, in effect, to categorize human experience. The task is difficult and its results are misleading. Yet, teachers are continuously required to both evaluate and grade. Making a clear distinction between these two activities is extremely important.

Evaluation is a crucial, ongoing, diagnostic process in which both teachers and students must engage in order to educate each other. The process is important to teachers because its results indicate how their teaching must be altered to help individual students or specific groups of students. Evaluation is an important activity to students because of the ongoing knowledge-of-results it affords. The process is crucial because the ability to accurately evaluate one's own work is prerequisite to the ultimate goal of all education—the development of the independent learner.

In contrast, grading is a social phenomenon with deep historic roots, the efficacy of which has long been disputed. Grades are labels applied in widely varying situations for a myriad of reasons to somehow describe human experience. Like all labels, grades have meaning only to the extent that a consensus exists on what they denote. No such agreement exists. Few attempt to defend rationales for grading students. The practice survives largely because of tradition, administrative expediency, and bureaucratic intransigence.

In the teaching laboratory, you can gain a great deal of direct experience in describing and evaluating through the feedback you are asked to provide to your colleagues about their teaching. Hopefully this experience will also improve your ability to evaluate the performance of your own students. Understanding a few fundamental concepts about the feedback procedure operating in the teaching laboratory can considerably enhance your ability to help your colleagues improve their teaching.

In general, the criteria upon which judgments will be made should be clear. This principle is easily understood, but less easily implemented. The best method presently available for communicating criteria to those whose performance will be evaluated requires stating the criteria for acceptable performance in terms of observable behavior (Mager, 1962). In other words, the chances of accomplishing a desired objective are enhanced if the evaluator and the evaluated agree *a priori* on the value of the objective and also on the observable evidence that will indicate its accomplishment. Such instructional objectives attempt to communicate concisely and accurately by avoiding the use of terms having many different interpretations (e.g., to know, to understand, to appreciate, etc.). When objectives are clear, evaluation becomes the relatively simple matter of judging whether or not the criterion for an acceptable performance has been met.

A well-written instructional objective satisfies four requirements necessary for the unambiguous communication of the criteria a teacher will use in evaluating his students' performances or, in the case of the teaching laboratory, your own and your colleagues' teaching. Of those listed, the last three are taken from Mager (1962, p. 12).

1. The objective identifies *who* must perform the act. In the case of the tasks in this manual, the who is you, the teacher.
2. The objective identifies the *terminal behavior* that is considered evidence that the desired learning has taken place and the objective has been accomplished. With respect to the tasks in this manual, the terminal behaviors are those of individuals who teach and are most often stated in terms of teaching behavior.

3. The objective attempts to define the desired behavior further by describing the important *conditions* under which the behavior will be expected to occur. The conditions under which you will perform the tasks in this manual are those present in the teaching laboratory (e.g., small number of students or role-playing colleagues, time limit, etc.). They are reasonably constant and, thus, are not restated for each objective found in this manual.

4. The objective specifies the *criteria of acceptable performance* by describing how well the learner must perform to be considered acceptable. Fulfilling this requirement is sometimes difficult if not dysfunctional with respect to the tasks in this manual. Teaching strategies are best considered in terms of their appropriateness or inappropriateness for specific situations rather than in terms of good or bad. Consequently, the objectives stated in this manual generally have rather imprecise criteria for *acceptable* performance but comparatively stringent criteria for *appropriate* performance in the specific situations created by each individual's teaching.

Evaluations of your colleagues' teaching should be based on how well they appropriately fulfill the objectives specified for that task. While you and your colleagues are encouraged to select topics that will allow you to apply all the required strategies of a specific task, finding one is sometimes difficult. Consider this in evaluating the appropriateness with which a specific teaching strategy has been used. The objectives for a task operationally attempt to define appropriateness for each of that task's teaching strategies. This should enhance the agreement between individuals offering feedback.

Because your descriptions and evaluations of teaching behavior do not necessarily suggest ways of improving that behavior, you and your colleagues will find more detailed feedback of great value in your attempts to improve your teaching. Thus, you may find it useful to supplement the general information elicited by the evaluation guides with oral and/or written comments conveying your more specific reactions to a microlesson. Common sense is a good guide as to what to say and/or write and how best to present it.

First, comments can refer to the general criteria upon which the task is based, or they can refer to the many other behaviors not being evaluated but still of crucial importance to effective teaching. Both are of value when they point the way to improved teaching behavior.

Second, everyone likes to hear about his strengths, but he is also interested in knowing his weaknesses. More precisely, he is interested in knowing *how* to overcome weak aspects of his teaching. Therefore, merging identifications of weaknesses with constructive suggestions for improvement is a highly desirable practice in the teaching laboratory as well as in the classroom. Strive for a healthy balance in your criticism (i.e., identify strengths as well as weaknesses) and your suggestions will not only be accepted but sought.

Third, avoid resorting to negative affect (feelings) and sarcasm (e.g., "you really stepped in the bucket when you . . ." or "that wasn't really teaching, but . . ."). One seldom slips into this mode of communication, but even small amounts of it can be very damaging to interpersonal relationships and to your credibility as an evaluator both in the teaching laboratory and in the classroom.

Fourth, work for quantity as well as quality in offering comments. Deciding which points will be most valuable to a colleague is often difficult. Giving him many comments enhances the possibility that you will hit upon a point of particular relevance to his present stage of development as a teacher. Providing comprehensive feedback can be a nuisance, but it can also aid you in developing the ability to isolate important parts from the whole, to diagnose weaknesses, and to prescribe alternatives—all of which are important attributes of effective teaching.

In summary, teachers must be able to provide useful feedback. The teaching laboratory offers you extensive experience in evaluating the performance of both your colleagues and yourself. Comprehensive feedback is valuable when it is both constructive and substantive. Feedback is of most educational value when it identifies a direction in which to alter behavior and suggests the means by which to do it.

2

*Process
Concerns*

4

Process as Content

The major purpose of this part of the manual is to introduce you to a set of strategies that will help you teach your students a set of process skills (ways of thinking) that are used in all subject areas. While it is true that each subject area has its own ways of thinking and methods by which new knowledge is continually generated, it is also true that all disciplines share a common core of investigative techniques.

That core may be thought of in simplest terms as the process of asking questions about the unknown and seeking answers to them. An example may illustrate the nature of this common pool of strategies. A botanist and a painter can look at the same flower and see two very different things. The botanist may see a type of inflorescence, a stamen of specific length, and a calyx with a unique structure. The artist may see hues and textures, forms and shadings. The flower is a different flower because the questions asked about it are different, because it has different unknowns. But both the botanist and the artist do ask questions; both have ways of seeking answers to them; both try to generalize those answers to other flowers or other parts of their experience; both are trying to make their unknown known. These similarities represent common problem-solving strategies.

To help students learn these ways of thinking is really to help them learn how to learn. The endeavor centers on the problem of teaching students how to formulate questions and then seek answers to them. Because process skills may be thought of as problem-solving strategies, and because problem-solving is most often taught via an inductive approach (i.e., discovery approach), these three concepts will be used interchangeably.

Problem-solving has been described and defined by many educators and psychologists and, with few exceptions, one finds a surprisingly high degree of agreement within their many formulations. In attempting a synthesis of these various views, Gagné (1966, p. 132) defines problem-solving as ". . . an inferred change in human capability that results in the acquisition of a generalizable rule which is novel to the individual, which cannot have been established by direct recall, and which can manifest itself in applicability to the solution of a class of problems."

Historical Background

Problem-solving is not a new concept. Plato and Aristotle both defined the act in much the same way as Gagné did. John Dewey's emphasis on process (learning by doing) gave renewed importance to process skills by making them the focus of most if not all learning. Misinterpretations of Dewey's work led to many unfortunate excesses. Freedom became license. Caring for children became not requiring them to do their best. Such excesses subsequently tarnished the reputations of the many schools successfully using Dewey's ideas. Largely as a reaction to these excesses, a much more essentialistic philosophy stressing "efficient, rigorous" expository techniques was spawned in the conservatism of the late 1940s and early 1950s and accelerated the already waning prominence of the practice of viewing process as valid content. In some quarters process concerns were even linked to "the communist conspiracy." Children who engaged in such informal kinds of learning supposedly would become intellectually flabby and be easy marks for a worldwide communist takeover.

Sputnik caused a complete reappraisal of the American educational system. This new and public examination resulted in a renewed emphasis on the teaching of process as a legitimate part of the content of courses (Bruner, 1960; Parker and Rubin, 1966). Numerous national curriculum projects began developing "new" ways of teaching specific subjects. If any one quality could possibly characterize all of them in their diversity it would be their attention to the teaching of process (Goodlad, et al., 1966). Most of the projects as yet have had only narrow dissemination. Postman and Weingartner (1969, p. 23) succinctly express the pessimism of a growing number of public school critics when they note that

> The most important intellectual ability man has yet developed—the art and science of asking questions—is not taught in school! Moreover, it is *not* "taught" in the most devastating way possible: by arranging the environment so that significant question asking is not valued. It is doubtful if you can think of many schools that include question asking or methods of inquiry, as a part of their curriculum.

Philosophical Rationale

John Gardner, former Secretary of Health, Education, and Welfare, once said, "too often we give our children cut flowers when we ought to be teaching them to grow their own." The philosophy behind teaching for problem-solving centers on this position. Knowledge is never increased by simply learning those things which are already known. Rather, the base of our present knowledge is extended by *using* knowledge to generate new knowledge. There is overwhelming agreement on this point. Disagreement arises with respect to the means employed to help students to do the generating. Some feel that knowledge will be generated naturally, that teaching the known culture is sufficient (Bestor, 1953, 1955; Lynd, 1953; Smith, 1949, 1956; Rickover, 1959, 1962, 1963). In their view, knowledge is a heritage that must be transmitted to the young. The perpetuation of the culture requires that that transmission be successful. The extent and diversity of the culture requires that that transmission also be efficient. Their position is that if a principle can be learned expositorily in one tenth the time of discovering it, then to learn it by the latter method is ludicrous because the student would be deprived of nine other principles which could be learned in the time necessary to "discover" one. Learning to discover is important, but it is far too time-consuming a procedure to merit having students simply rediscover that which others already know.

Others feel that this position is only part of the story, that students must not only learn how to know, but how to think or transform information (Piaget, 1968). To *become* a scientist, musician, or mathematician, one must *think* like a scientist, musician, or mathematician (Bruner, 1960; Combs, 1962). To do this effectively, one must teach students how to apply that common core of problem-solving strategies to a particular subject area rather than leaving the development and transfer of those strategies to chance. This manual adopts this position.

What Knowledge Is of Most Worth?

Schools are very cognitive, knowledge-oriented institutions. The extent to which they should be that way is debatable, but that issue will be discussed in Chapter 10. For now, simply note that excluding extracurricular and quasi-extracurricular activities (the "soft," less "important" subjects), schools are almost wholly committed to the task of having their students "acquire" as much knowledge as they can. The goal may be worthy, but it is seldom achieved because of the constrained definition schools give to knowledge.

Schools have made knowledge that which is most concrete, most unambiguous, most *right*. In other words, knowledge is what can be codified in a traditional, objective, paper and pencil test. Questions involving simple (and sometimes verbatim) recall are very easy to construct, evaluate, and grade. That the mastery of this kind of knowledge constitutes a large majority of the learning schools require of their clientele is well documented, but you need go no further than your own experience as a student for evidence supporting the claim.

Children enter school as vital, enthusiastic questioners and quickly learn that there are questions and then there are questions. The reward system of the school centers on finding answers to the teacher's questions and finding those answers becomes a student's major goal. Holt (1964) makes a distinction between producers and thinkers. Thinkers are means (process) oriented while producers are goal (product) oriented. If rewards are given only for products, students will resort to most any behavior including fishing for hints and cheating. In other words, they become producers. Thinking is seldom the easiest path to the answer, and because it is not, it is a seldom-traveled one, especially when the answer requires a student to do little more than simply remember.

Schools do not have to be this way. Alternatives do exist. Processes can be goals as easily as products. The next chapter will deal with *how* to plan lessons with process goals.

Bruner (1961) reinforces *why* a teacher should plan for process by citing four advantages to discovery learning. They represent an excellent synthesis of the conclusions drawn from the research on process. When used appropriately, the discovery method increases intellectual potency (the expectation of success), intrinsic motivation (an interest in learning for learning's sake), the learning of the heuristics of discovery (the strategies used in solving problems), and the amount of information actually retained (learning). Perhaps the crucial factor here is appropriateness. Various teaching strategies are usually best viewed as being appropriate or inappropriate to specific situations. Here, as elsewhere in teaching, few recipes exist. When used appropriately, confronting students with lifelike problems to solve is a powerful teaching strategy. Obviously, process concerns do not negate the student's need to acquire important aspects of the culture. They simply put that need in its proper perspective. Nor is the teaching of process a panacea for all educational ills; it is a very important additional set of strategies a teacher will find useful as he attempts to develop independence in his students.

The Problem-Solving Act

The act of problem-solving is generally seen as having three rather distinct phases. Borton (1970, p. 88) proposes a very simple information-processing model incorporating these phases which are labeled *"What?"*, *"So What?"*, and *"Now What?"*. The *"What?"* phase involves the "sensing out of response, actual effect, and intended effect." One might term it an encounter with incongruity. The incongruity is the problem. Before one can begin solving it, one must have a very clear idea of just what the problem is. What are its characteristics and limits? What are the relevant aspects (information) in the total environment?

The second phase, *"So What?"*, is the process of "transforming that information into immediately relevant patterns of meaning." Once the nature of the problem *("What?")* is well defined, the natural consequence is to begin searching for a solution. At this point, one either formally or informally begins to hypothesize or guess possible solutions for the problem and then attempts to verify which alternative is the most plausible. Several of the hypotheses may be partial explanations of the principle necessary for solving the problem. One will most likely be or seem best. Verification of the correct guess may proceed in any fashion from blind trial and error to a rigorously controlled experimental situation (which is really only another kind of trial and error).

Once a tentative principle or solution rule is arrived at, a second type of verification begins and this action marks the beginning of the *"Now What?"* phase in which decisions are made on "how to act on the best alternative and reapply it in other situations." If the solution is in fact a valid identification of the crucial principle, it should be generalizable. Satisfaction of this phase of the problem-solving situation reconciles the original incongruity and terminates the process, allowing the individual to direct his attention to other activities.

Each of these three phases will be the focus for one of the following three microteaching tasks in which the strategies involved in teaching each phase will be described in detail.

5

Planning for Process

Every teacher wants to teach his students to think. The commitment is universal, even if so noble a purpose is regularly thwarted in practice. An early obstruction to the facilitation of process outcomes is the considerable problem of creating settings in which process concerns can easily be emphasized. Many difficulties surround your aspirations to teach for process; and while a chronicle of such barriers is not in order, a discussion of the most crucial ones is important if your commitment is to result in action.

First, you likely are a victim of your experience. Schools make little systematic effort to teach process. More than a decade has passed since the first major curriculum projects emphasizing process concerns were developed and disseminated. Yet a recent nationwide study revealed that these curricula have received only piecemeal acceptance in our schools (Silberman, 1970). Undergraduate education at the college level fares little better (Schwab, 1969). The large lecture halls of our universities are far more conducive to presenting their inmates with arrays of facts and relationships than to engaging them in the vagaries of inquiry and discovery. Modeling is a potent learning strategy, finely honed in a person's infancy and relied on often unconsciously thereafter. If you are human, you model, and because you model, you will tend to teach as you were taught. Unless you have had uncommonly good luck, your schooling has provided you with very few process-oriented models.

Second, teaching for process outcomes works best when it deals with the basic principles and assumptions that support the thinking in your subject area, principles and assumptions that *you* have long since encountered, internalized, and come to take for granted. Try conceptualizing the increasingly specialized training you have had in your discipline as something resembling an inverted funnel. As a beginner, you entered the lower end, the funnel's wide mouth. You had much latitude in your behavior; you could move about in a comparatively unrestricted manner, accumulating the basic foundation of facts, skills, and attitudes upon which the discipline is built. But increased experience moved you further up the funnel, bringing increased constraints upon your behavior. As your needs and interests became increasingly esoteric, the original wonder and naivete of the uninitiated became correspondingly more difficult to recapture until the view back down the funnel became obscured.

Planning for process is remembering what it is like in the bottom of the funnel. It is rediscovering the general principles that constitute the bedrock of your discipline and developing situations in which your students can encounter incongruities or confront lifelike problem situations which may be reconciled or solved only by uncovering and applying those principles. In actual teaching situations, process settings can be generated naturally by allowing your students the freedom of the funnel mouth. Here, planning for process becomes recognizing and taking advantage of spontaneous events with process potential. The time limit constraints of the teaching laboratory make this approach unfeasible. An atmosphere of freedom is not established in eight days, let alone eight minutes.

Sources do exist which can help you re-establish your view of the funnel mouth. Instructors and/or colleagues are obvious ones. Brainstorming (sharing ideas) for topics and approaches with other teachers in your subject area is often productive. Using the same process with a cross-disciplinary team can generate many fresh perspectives (e.g., a physicist's view of music or a home economist's view of chemistry). Over and above the unique view fostered by their own specializations, people outside your discipline are also more likely to have the perspective of the uninitiated layman, the freedom of the funnel mouth.

Defining Process Objectives and Designing Instruction

Planning for process requires that you understand the requirements of the task you are setting for your students. What kinds of knowledge, attitudes, and skills are prerequisite to it? Will your students, with their various attention spans, be able to persist long enough to solve the problem? Are they being asked to perform any operations they have never before performed? Asking such questions and seeking answers to them are the rudimentary operations entailed in what is commonly termed a "task analysis." Thoroughly analyzing a learning task is a complex procedure, especially when designing programmed instruction where this activity is crucial. Seldom, however, will you need to operate with a programmer's degree of sophistication in planning microlessons. In most cases, some simple guidelines should suffice.

To reiterate, your students solve problems by acquiring (ideally, discovering) the principle or generalization which explains an entire set of situations to which the problem just solved belongs. In other words, it is the process of finding a general answer to a set of specific questions. Analyzing the task you are setting for your students involves starting with the principle you wish them to learn and working backward step by step until you have a complete picture of the learning processes your students will need to use to get from where they are (their entering behavior) to where they are going (the instructional objective—acquisition of the principle). Identifying and helping your students satisfy prerequisites takes on importance if you hope to have them function independently during the problem-solving activity. When students lack a prerequisite, they find themselves in the position of having to resort to artificial means for solving a problem (e.g., rote learning, blind trial and error, etc.). Try to consider such problems as you plan your microlesson. Try to anticipate where pitfalls for your students may lie and prepare to bridge or circumvent them. Avoid two pervasive planning errors: do not assume too much of your students, and do not overlook crucial stages in their progress toward the solution to the problem.

Subject Areas and Their Traditional Process Emphases

Planning problems vary with the kinds of questions and means of solving them that characterize each subject area. For example, the teaching of process is stressed in some subject areas (e.g., the sciences) more than others. Because of their history of concern with process, these subject areas can be collectively referred to as process-oriented subject areas. Upon inspection, two additional classes of instructional orientation also emerge. Several subject areas share an emphasis of verbal learning and can therefore be collectively referred to as verbally-oriented subject areas. Several other subject areas share an emphasis on skill acquisition and can therefore be collectively referred to as skill-oriented subject areas.

The categories are admittedly arbitrary. They may be effectively challenged on several points, not the least of which is the fact that the teaching of every subject area is concerned with presenting components of all three of the realms identified. The categories are simply a convenience, allowing the discussion of the planning problems of each special subject area to be supplanted by a more general discussion of the planning problems common to a group of them. The major criterion for categorizing each subject area centers on the question of which classification best describes the general instructional approach most often used in teaching it.

Process-oriented subject areas. Mathematics, the natural sciences, and the social sciences are the subject areas described by this category. Teachers in these subject areas have traditionally displayed considerably more commitment to process concerns than teachers in most other subject areas, perhaps because the investigative techniques of at least the natural and social sciences are more visible and often glamorized.

Most of the process-laden national curriculum projects developed thus far deal with these subject areas, perhaps indicating that they represent those subjects in which process concerns are most easily identified and satisfied. The "new" mathematics is designed to continually confront students with basic mathematical relationships and concepts as they work problems. Dozens of simulations and games allow social science students to become mayors, ecologists, black people (or white people), or whatever—engaged in lifelike problem-solving situations. The routine science laboratory experiment with its preset questions has been replaced by exercises that require the development of questioning strategies or basic discrimination skills. In general, when the teaching task involves planning for process, teachers of these process-oriented subject areas have a comparatively easy lot.

Verbally-oriented subject areas. Drama, English, the foreign languages, journalism, and speech are the subject areas described by this category. A central objective of each is the improvement of some form of verbal communication. They are consequently concerned with skill development, but of a very special kind. Verbal learning relies heavily on modeling behavior. Even after twelve years of formal training in English grammar, a student probably still speaks the language with the mannerisms and inflections of his parents.

Much foreign language instruction is highly structured drill. The situation requires that the student's need (to learn a foreign language) be compatible with the teacher's expertise (to teach that language). The relationship collapses whenever that compatibility no longer exists (Benne, 1970). Here, motivating becomes creating a need. One way to create needs is to help your students see your subject area from a new perspective. In the case of a foreign language, the new perspective might be that of a native speaker. In the case of other verbally-oriented subject areas, it could involve helping your students attack lifelike problems as an actor, linguist, journalist, etc. might. Again, the task is to help your students think and solve problems as persons in your subject area would by introducing him to its basic principles via process approaches.

Skill-oriented subject areas.   Art, business, health and physical education, home economics, industrial and vocational education, and music are the subject areas described by this category. They are so classified because a predominant mode of instruction for each involves helping students acquire psychomotor (manipulative) skills. They also contain considerable verbal emphasis, and of course, each includes a set of unique heuristics (ways of thinking) that constitute each subject area's process concerns. Some involve esthetics. In each case, however, the *primary* instructional goal of each (at least as they are taught in schools) is the acquisition of skills.

Modeling and trial and error drill are major instructional modes used in skill-oriented subject areas. Thus, the teacher-expertise/student-need relationship again becomes a concern. Working with lifelike problem situations is an ideal format in which to teach for process outcomes, especially in those subject areas that have a strong vocational emphasis. Again, each subject area has its basic principles, concepts, and relationships. Solving problems involving them is one more way to build interest in these subjects and to build an emphasis on process.

Two examples may clarify this point. Public school music is generally equated with performance groups (bands, orchestras, and choirs). Performance skills are acquired in rehearsals for concerts, but a musician is far more than a quasi-automaton who can follow directions and do as he is told; he can generate new, reasoned interpretations of established works or perhaps create new ones. The complete musician thinks like a musician. He has a command of the basic precepts upon which music is built. In other words, he is able to independently initiate processes as well as generate products.

Physical education has been labeled anti-intellectual, but physiology, gaming strategies, and the expressiveness and emotional release of bodily movement are hardly anti-intellectual. If a student is to comprehend or even perceive the events occurring as he performs or watches others perform physical acts, he needs to have ways of thinking of those acts. How the game is played does become more important than who won or lost. Process approaches can aid the attainment of this objective.

Example Process Approaches For All Subject Areas

One problem mentioned earlier that makes the planning of process approaches difficult is the absence of models. The printed page is not an effective medium for filling this void, but these examples are intended as stimuli to your own creative efforts rather than as a catalog from which to select your microlesson topics. Although only two examples are given for each subject area, many of those listed can be easily adapted to other areas or to other age levels (e.g., from secondary to elementary).

Elementary Level

Level: Primary grades
Topic: Grouping objects.
Basic Concept: Things can be classified in many ways.
Processes Required: Discriminating, classifying, and categorizing strategies.
Approach: Give students a large pool of diverse objects and ask them to find as many ways that they are alike or different as they can.

Level: Primary grades
Topic: Lost in the city.
Basic Concept: One can obtain information and help through questioning.
Processes Required: Questioning, developing a hierarchy of contingencies.
Approach: The student has become separated from his parents on a shopping expedition. What should he do?

Level: Intermediate grades
Topic: Building a Stonehenge arch.
Basic Concept: The inclined plane is a basic machine. Different cultures have different values.
Processes Required: Formulating and verifying hypotheses.
Approach: Set scene and constraints. The students are the men of Stonehenge. "How can you raise this huge stone arch?" (see p. 59).

Level:	Intermediate grades
Topic:	Storytelling.
Basic Concept:	Language has severe limitations.
Processes Required:	Listening, describing, analyzing, and introspecting.
Approach:	Whisper to one student a very short but rather involved story containing several characters. He whispers the story to another student and so on. After several students have told the story, have the last student tell the story to the entire class, then retell the original story. "What has happened and why? Can it be avoided?"

Process-Oriented Subject Areas

Subject Area:	Mathematics
Topic:	Developing a number system.
Basic Concept:	Zero serves a crucial function by establishing place (i.e., units, tens, hundreds, etc.).
Processes Required:	Formulating number systems (hypothesizing) and checking out their usefulness (verifying hypotheses).
Approach:	"Develop a number system without using a zero or any other symbol that represents 'nothing'."

Subject Area:	Mathematics
Topic:	Measuring the height of an unreachable object.
Basic Concept:	Lifelike problems can be solved using trigonometric relationships.
Processes Required:	Setting up problems, measuring, applying principles, computing results.
Approach:	"Given a tape measure and a surveyor's transit, how would you go about measuring the height of the school's flagpole (or the old oak tree)?"

Subject Area:	Science
Topic:	Human evolution.
Basic Concept:	Principles of adaptation.
Processes Required:	Extrapolating, hypothesizing, identifying cause-effect relationships.
Approach:	Identify some of the human organs that are presently outmoded. "Assuming that man will continue to adapt to his environment, draw a picture of man as he might appear a half million years from now." Discuss these pictures (see p. 74).

Subject Area:	Science
Topic:	Black box experiment.
Basic Concept:	The nature of science.
Processes Required:	Perceiving, hypothesizing and verifying hypotheses, introspecting.
Approach:	Give students sealed boxes containing various objects. Without opening the boxes, they must decide what is in each. Introspect the processes they go through.

Subject Area: Social science
Topic: Group decision-making.
Basic Concept: Various factors affect how a group makes a decision and what decision they make.
Processes Required: Decision-making, valuing, various survival strategies, introspecting.
Approach: The class is stranded on the moon. They have a list of fifteen items and must establish, both individually and as a group, priority rankings for the items. "How did you arrive at decisions? How do your individual lists compare with the one for the group?" (see p. 71).

Subject Area: Social science
Topic: Prejudice.
Basic Concept: Debilitating qualities of prejudice.
Processes Required: Analyzing behavior and feelings causing it.
Approach: The class continues as usual except that one segment of it is discriminated against because of some physical trait (e.g., hair color). After sufficient time has elapsed, process the experiences that have accumulated.

Verbally-Oriented Subject Areas

Subject Area: Drama/Speech
Topic: Hamlet
Basic Concept: Character relationships and the effect of plot.
Processes Required: Identifying alternative interpretations (hypotheses) and verifying the "most valid" one.
Approach: Describe continuing controversy over the "correct" interpretation of Hamlet. "What are some ways of viewing the melancholy Dane? Which seems best? Why?"

Subject Area: Drama/Speech
Topic: The silent language.
Processes Required: Perceiving, discriminating, analyzing, and introspecting.
Approach: Show films or videotapes of people talking with sound turned off. "What do their nonverbal actions convey? What kinds of nonverbal behavior communicate best? Which are most misleading? Why did you choose to focus on these behaviors rather than others?"

Subject Area: English
Topic: Character development.
Basic Concept: Social relationships of characters.
Processes Required: Analyzing.
Approach: Explain sociograms. Ask students to build a sociogram of the *Peanuts* comic strip characters. "How many ways can information

about a character's social status be conveyed?" (By what he says about himself, by how he acts, etc.). What kinds of information did you use to build your sociogram?"

Subject Area:	English
Topic:	Poetry.
Basic Concept:	One connotative meaning of "poetic."
Processes Required:	Analyzing, interpreting, and empathizing.
Approach:	"Why does one man write poetry while another does not? Why does a man become a poet? Why not communicate in more conventional ways? Does poetry have any specific power?"

Subject Area:	Foreign languages
Topic:	Influence of one language upon another.
Basic Concept:	The "borrowing" nature of English.
Processes Required:	Identifying examples.
Approach:	"Has anyone ever milked a beef? Or held a young mutton in his lap?" Explain influence of the Norman invasions on English language (French became the fashionable dinner language, and thus, meats were called by their French names at the table). "Can anyone identify some words that English has borrowed from other languages recently—say the last ten years?"

Subject Area:	Foreign languages
Topic:	Translating a poem.
Basic Concept:	The difficulties involved in translating connotative meanings.
Processes Required:	Translating, hypothesizing (suggesting alternative phrases), and verifying hypotheses (selecting the best phrase).
Approach:	The class is asked to translate a short poem in English into a foreign language. Not only must the translation be accurate regarding denotative problems, but it must also be "poetic" by trying to maintain the connotations implied in the original poem. The students suggest alternative ways of expressing each phrase and then select the best translation.

Subject Area:	Journalism
Topic:	Headlines.
Basic Concept:	Headlines should motivate the reader to read the article.
Processes Required:	Analyzing and evaluating.
Approach:	"Which of these headlines is best for the story you have just read? Why? What do you value in a headline?" (see p. 62).

Subject Area:	Journalism
Topic:	Copywriting, reporting.
Basic Concept:	Concise communication.
Processes Required:	Perceiving, analyzing, and synthesizing.

Approach:	Prearrange a traumatic incident with one student (e.g., quarrel and throw him out of the room) and spring it on the class. "You've just seen a news event. Give me a paragraph on it for the school newspaper in five minutes." Discuss and critique the products.

Skill-Oriented Subject Areas

Subject Area:	Art
Topic:	The function of color.
Basic Concept:	Colors depict moods.
Processes Required:	Perceiving and analyzing.
Approach:	Show several Picassos (blue period). "How would these paintings change if we could take the blue out of them?" Follow the same procedure with Rembrandt and black.

Subject Area:	Art
Topic:	Definition of art.
Basic Concept:	Bad art is still art. Art's fundamental definition should not be contingent upon quality.
Processes Required:	Discriminating, analyzing, hypothesizing, and verifying hypotheses.
Approach:	"What is art?" Collect several definitions. "Which do you like most? Why?" After sufficient processing, take a controversial stand. "I don't like any of those definitions. Art is simply *anything* that is man-made." Defend yourself.

Subject Area:	Business
Topic:	Decision-making.
Basic Concept:	Examine priorities before acting.
Processes Required:	Hypothesizing and verifying hypotheses.
Approach:	"The boss is on a fishing trip and is unreachable. An important matter suddenly arises requiring an immediate decision." Relate all important details. "What do you do? How do you proceed?"

Subject Area:	Business
Topic:	Applying for a secretarial job.
Basic Concept:	Criteria determining a good secretary.
Processes Required:	Perceiving, analyzing, and evaluating.
Approach:	Provide students with the application data for five recent high school graduates, all seeking a job you describe. They are given application forms, examples of typing and shorthand, a picture of the applicant, and a tape recording of the job interview. "Which one gets the job and why? Could you beat the winner out for this job? Where must you improve to do it?"

Subject Area: Health/Physical Education
Topic: Individual physical fitness.
Basic Concept: Physiological needs vary with the individual.
Processes Required: Analyzing and synthesizing.
Approach: Have students make an extensive list of their own body measurements. "Where do you need to reproportion your measurements? Design a conditioning program that will do it. After you've finished, compare it with the programs other students develop. See if you can draw any conclusions from the similarities and differences you find."

Subject Area: Health/Physical Education
Topic: Building a game plan.
Basic Concept: Winning involves applying force at your opponents' vulnerable points.
Processes Required: Identifying relationships, analyzing, and hypothesizing.
Approach: Give students a detailed scouting report on an upcoming hypothetical opponent. Also detail the strengths and weaknesses of the students' team. "What will be your plan of attack? Why? What if that doesn't work? Why did you decide on that course of action?"

Subject Area: Home Economics
Topic: Budgets.
Basic Concept: Budgeting requires establishing priorities.
Processes Required: Discriminating, analyzing, and synthesizing.
Approach: Give teams of students extensive food price lists, and a set amount of food money. "Plan a week's meals for this family. How did you make your selections? Why didn't you buy any _____? Why is this the best possible diet?"

Subject Area: Home Economics
Topic: Fashion.
Basic Concept: The nature and cause of fashion.
Processes Required: Identifying relationships, analyzing, hypothesizing, and verifying hypotheses.
Approach: "What is a fashion? How does it differ from a fad? Why does something become fashionable? Does that make any sense?"

Subject Area: Industrial/Vocational Education
Topic: Woodworking
Basic Concept: Wood has a unique set of properties.
Processes Involved: Perceiving and analyzing.
Approach: "What can you do with wood? What can't you do? Is wood consistent? Why not? What problems have you encountered thus far as you've worked with wood?"

Subject Area:	Industrial/Vocational Education
Topic:	Production techniques.
Basic Concept:	Many variables affect production procedures.
Processes Involved:	Ordering, analyzing, and synthesizing.
Approach:	"Here's an iron casting that we have to turn into this finished product. Set up the most efficient procedure for doing it."

Subject Area:	Music
Topic:	Analysis of form.
Basic Concept:	Repetition (the recurrence of thematic material) is a major determinant of form.
Processes Involved:	Perceiving, identifying relationships, recognizing recapitulations, and analyzing.
Approach:	Play a short, early classic period piece (e.g., a rondo) for the students. "How many different musical ideas (or phrases) did you hear? Were any used more than once? Did you begin to anticipate their recurrence? Why?"

Subject Area:	Music
Topic:	Musical interpretation.
Basic Concept:	The performer plays an important role in communicating the composer's intent.
Processes Involved:	Perceiving, discriminating, analyzing, and evaluating.
Approach:	Play the same segment from several recorded renditions of a standard piece from the repertoire. "Can all these performances be conveying the composer's intent? What *is* a composer's intent when he writes music? What is the performer's responsibility?"

6

Role-Playing for Process [1]

Microteaching was conceived within the context of a summer clinic which hired children and adolescents to be students for a group of graduate students preparing to become teaching interns. Using real students obviously maximizes realism, but the funds and logistics required to carry on such an endeavor steadily increase as the number of teachers increases. The limited availability of students during the regular school year when most teacher education takes place poses an additional handicap. As a result of such problems, most adaptations of microteaching substitute role-playing peers for actual students. Teachers working in such programs may find some of the following suggestions useful in preparing themselves to carry out the important charge of role-playing realistic students for their colleagues.

---

[1] This chapter may be skipped if you will be teaching to real students rather than role-playing peers.

Role-Playing Guidelines

First, assuming the role of a specific person is a generally desirable strategy. In many cases that person can be you at an earlier age.

Example: Be an average tenth-grader in English.

For a start, try to think back to your own tenth grade English class. Think of your teacher, your classmates, and your collective attitudes toward your teacher, each other, English, and school in general. Did the class easily volunteer information or was it reticent? Was your class really average, or did most of the students in it go on to college?

Secondly, there are times when role-playing yourself at a younger age will not solve the problem. This situation occurs when the assumed role is outside your range of experience.

Example: (A problem for a woman) Role-play a hyperactive boy in an eighth grade physical education class.

Example: (A problem for a man) Be a junior girl with low aspirations in a home economics (cooking) class.

In such cases, try to remember a particular student you went to school with who would fit the description. Try to be that person. Sometimes a composite of two or more persons works best. Assume the role that seems natural and exemplary to you. Your task may also be complicated by the fact that you have never had the subject taught to you. In such a case, you may consider yourself a student with learning problems. Use whatever other devices you find helpful.

Thirdly, additional problems arise when you are asked to role-play a primary age child or a slow learner. Not only does the knowledge base of such a child grossly differ from your own but also his cognitive processes (ways of thinking).

Example: Be a first-grader.

Extensive, direct experience with many small children is perhaps the best preparation for role-playing this situation, especially if that experience is augmented by reading on the cognitive processes of small children (e.g., Piaget, Montessori). As an alternative to such experience, you might attempt to simulate a young relative or neighbor. Again, use any device that helps you get into the role.

As a teacher, you can help your "students" be more realistic by structuring their roles for them. Taking a moment to carefully describe the behavior you would like from them, the background they have or do not have and their interests and attitudes before you start your microlesson, can greatly assist your colleagues' role-playing efforts. You may even wish to direct individuals to play specific roles.

> *Example:* Jerry, you have something of a bad attitude. Martha, you're my pet; you do your best to please me—all the time. Jan, you have very little interest in school. The rest of you are just average ability, socially-minded adolescents.

Role-playing is not difficult. The hardest part of the task may well be avoiding the temptation to overplay your part. If you need convincing evidence of the reality role-playing peers can bring to microlessons, you need only look ahead to the example microlessons on pages 48–51, 59–65, and 71–77. All the "students" in these microlessons were undergraduate students in teacher education.

7

TASK TWO
What?
Encountering Incongruity

Task One provided you with very little structure. Indeed, one of its purposes was to allow you to observe how you teach when you are on your own. The rest of the tasks in this manual excepting the last one will require you to teach in specific ways. Task Two, for example, asks you to set the stage for learning. For problem-solving to be a useful instructional strategy, it is important that students *and* teacher get started correctly.

Creating Problem Situations

Your overall goal for this microteaching task is to create in your students the unsettled state that results when they experience an event that either seemingly contradicts or violates a "truth" they have consciously or unconsciously accepted, or a problem incident that is sufficiently life-like to make problem-solving a valid activity for them. Some examples of each type or situation may best illustrate what the task involves.

Creating Incongruity

Example: Several problems such as 6 + 11 = 20 and 22 − 14 = 3 create incongruity for a student who does not know the principle of base. The problem: Find out why the arithmetic in these and other similar problems is "correct."

Example: A strip of paper defying gravity when a stream of air is blown over it is incongruous to a student who does not know Bernoulli's principle. The problem: Why does the paper rise?

Example: The teacher asks, "What is art?" After several students attempt definitions, the teacher states that art is *anything* that is manmade; incongruity is created. The problem: Each student must seek a definition of art with which he feels secure.

Creating A Lifelike Situation

Example: The teacher describes the closing seconds of a basketball game in which the students are behind by two points. The description includes all pertinent information—the abilities of individual players on each team, the position of the ball on the court, the defense to expect, etc. The problem: Come up with the strategy most likely to tie or win the game.

Example: The teacher has several piles of chocolate chip cookies. She explains that each pile of cookies is lacking one of the recipe's ingredients. The problem: Determine what is missing in each batch.

Example: The students are divided into seven groups, each representing a fictional country. All the geographies and relative military strengths are described. The problem: Each country must formulate its own foreign policy, seek out those alliances it deems necessary, and decide on war or peace.[1]

Specifically, the task involves several basic planning and teaching strategies. The planning strategies include finding an appropriate problem for your students to solve and analyzing the task with which they will be confronted in solving it (see Chapter 5). The teaching strategies you are asked to use include assessing your students' entering behavior (readiness to learn), teaching them any capabilities they do not have that are prerequisite to an ability to solve the problem, and confronting them with sufficient incongruity or with a sufficiently likelike problem to stimulate problem-solving activity.

Assessing Entering Behavior

One of your tasks is to determine, early in the microlesson, whether or not your students possess the prerequisite capabilities you identified

[1] See Hyman (1970, p. 186) for a detailed description of this simulation game.

in planning your lesson. Examples of prerequisite cognitive capabilities might include a *knowledge* of the Bill of Rights, the ability to *translate* a verbal problem into an algebraic equation, or the ability to *extrapolate* present events into the future. Some prerequisite affective capabilities might be the harboring of an unconscious *prejudice,* or a *belief* in a specific value. Examples of some psychomotor capabilities might be the ability to *touch* specific keys of the typewriter without looking at them, the ability to *dribble* a basketball left-handed, or the ability to *perform* an A-flat arpeggio at a specific tempo.

A lack of a prerequisite ability may be caused by at least three factors. Obviously, one factor may be that the student simply has not learned something to which he was previously exposed. Second, the ability may be missing because of his sociocultural background. Millions of "disadvantaged" students have trouble in our middleclass-oriented schools because the presence of certain entering behaviors they do not possess is assumed. Tragically, most schools also assume the *absence* of many highly developed abilities which are not normally part of the middle-class child's repertoire. Third, a student may not have reached the stage of development necessary for the acquisition of certain abilities. While this problem is especially important at the elementary level, development does not stop there. For example, the attitudes arising from post-pubescent heterosexual relationships may be essential to certain topics you wish to teach.

Note that intelligence is not included in this list. Innate ability is obviously an important learning factor, but over-reliance on the significance of the intelligence quotient causes problems too. Research indicates that teacher expectation is a powerful determinant of the level of achievement reached by students (Rosenthal, 1968; Rosenthal and Jacobson, 1968a, 1968b). It suggests that a student's achievement increases significantly when his teacher is led to believe that he is more able than his past work indicates. In most cases, the fairest attitude to take is that students have the innate *capacity* to do the work and that any deficiency in capabilities is a result of the *environmental factors* discussed above and can probably be remedied *if* all the missing skills prerequisite to a task can be identified and enough time is available to teach them. Identification of missing prerequisites is important at this point because it is usually anticlimatic to stumble upon one in the heat of problem-solving activity and have to digress long enough to remedy the situation.

Teaching Missing Prerequisites

If missing prerequisites are identified, teaching them before the students are confronted with the problem is most important. Many studies

(Scandura, 1966a, 1966b, 1966c; Scandura and Behr, 1966; Amster, 1966; and Gagné, 1962, 1964) indicate that a student's premature entrance into a problem-solving situation results in his being generally ineffective in handling the problem in any productive manner. As a result, little learning takes place. Missing prerequisites can be identified and taught by having students summarize important previous learning. Students can be questioned to determine if they can identify crucial relationships or use basic concepts. By all means, though, avoid the stock "Do you understand . . . ?" that can be answered with an ambiguous and often misleading nod of the head. If the problem selected is fairly appropriate to the capabilities of your students, teaching prerequisites should be a simple matter. If gross deficiencies are apparent, confrontation with the problem would best be postponed until a later, more appropriate time.

Presenting the Problem

Once the previous requirements have been met, the stage is set for the presentation of the problem. Incongruities and lifelike problem situations arouse curiosity.

Regarding incongruity, Berlyne (1954) and Festinger (1957) identify two factors determining the strength of the conflict causing it. The first is the degree of disagreement between two existing events. Take for example a situation in which a student believes strongly in some principle, be it the law of gravity, his own lack of racial prejudice, that Bach's music is unenjoyable to him, or any other well-established value or fact he holds to be true. Information in conflict with this belief, be it a strip of paper defying gravity as an airstream is directed over it, a personal decision based on a prejudice, or a popular adaptation of a Bach theme by the Swingle Singers, creates a curiosity-arousing incongruity. The amount of curiosity aroused is in part a product of the *amount of conflict* between these two events.

The second factor determining the degree of curiosity aroused is the *relative strength* of the two events. If one belief or the other can be easily rejected, little curiosity results. If, however, both must be held to tenaciously, great conflict can be created and with it activity aimed at reducing the incongruity. For example, a student must be able to easily reject either his belief that the laws of gravity are constant or his belief that seeing is believing for the rising paper *not* to be a curiosity-arousing event. He must be able to easily reject either his belief that racial prejudice is debilitating or his belief that the decision-making process he just engaged in was a realistic simulation in order for information indicating that his decisions consistently favor one race *not* to be curiosity-arousing.

Similarly, a student must be able to easily reject either his belief that "longhaired" music is dry and boring or his belief that the label on the record he just listened to is telling the truth for a thoroughly enjoyable musical experience with Bach not to be a curiosity-arousing event. Such events are informative; they force us to expand our awareness and re-examine our generalizations. Curiosity-arousing events are also enjoyable. Few feelings are more stimulating than mystery, the stock-in-trade of the magician. In effect, you are being asked to "trick" your students into a learning situation. This then is your final objective for this micro-lesson—arouse sufficient curiosity to stimulate problem-solving behavior.

Regarding lifelike problem situations, credibility is important. The problem must be sufficiently realistic for your students to view it as more than game-playing. *They must also view themselves as capable of solving the problem.* Incongruity is aroused when they are confronted with a reality they feel they should be capable of understanding, but for some reason, temporarily cannot. To avoid trying to solve the problem, they must reject either the reality of the situation or downgrade their own capabilities. Your task is to insure that both alternatives are out of the question for your students. Solving the problem must be the most comfortable way for them to eliminate incongruity.

You are not required to go beyond this point for this task. Time requirements will probably prohibit actual entry into the problem-solving situation. If the assessment of entering behavior, the teaching of missing prerequisites, and the presentation of the problem take less time than anticipated, you may elect to either end your lesson at that point or enter into actual problem-solving activity.

Example Microlessons

Microteaching can be considered real teaching only in a very limited sense. It is, rather, an effective simulation that has a unique set of constraints not found in real teaching. In terms of fulfilling the very complex tasks described in this manual, the most difficult of these constraints is the pressure of time under which you are asked to teach.

The idea that this does not affect your teaching is absurd—it very much does. For example, you will find yourself "guiding" discovery, "structuring" problem situations, and in general being more directive than you would like to be—and more so than this manual's tasks ask you to be—simply because the pressure of time demands it. Try to keep this contextual characteristic of the teaching laboratory in mind as you evaluate your microlessons and those of your colleagues. An important question that should be asked repeatedly is, "How would I have taught this microlesson differently had this been a 'real' teaching situation?" This is also an important question to ask as you review the example microlessons included in this and the following two process-teaching tasks. While these are *example* microlessons, they may not be *exemplary*.

They are not ideal models for two reasons. Many microlessons do not offer opportunities for all the objectives for a particular task to be satisfied, even though the lesson may be very appropriately taught (see p. 18). For example, a microlesson might require such minimal competencies that very little assessing of entering behavior is needed, but the assessment that is made is nevertheless appropriate for that microlesson with that group of students.

The example microlessons are also not ideal models because they are, in fact, sparingly edited typescripts of actual microlessons taught by teachers like yourself, grappling for the first time with the problems of a strange role (teacher) in a semi-alien environment (the teaching laboratory).

Kindergarten

Dialogue	*Commentary*
T: All right class, please clear your desks. (pause) Anyone know what a specimen is?	T. begins assessing entering behavior through questioning.
S: (Several incorrect guesses are offered.)	
T: Well, that's a very difficult word, but a specimen is a true-to-life example of something. It's a word used in science and I have a specimen for each of you. (Opens small carton)	
S: Worms!	
S: Ugh! (Series of varied exclamations from class)	
T: (Gives each student a worm) You don't have to touch it, just keep it on the paper towel.	
S: (Much comment from class, teacher allows initial excitement to subside)	T. permits S. to do their own experimentation and manipulation, but observes them closely as they do so. Later, T. decides they are ready to continue.
T: Okay class, now while you look at your worms, I'm going to ask you some questions about them. Asher, can you tell me anything special about your earthworm?	T. begins establishing a learning set—describing worms.
S: He's got dirt on him.	

Dialogue

T: What is he doing compared to Joan's earthworm?

S: He's a . . . They are both doing the same thing.

T: And what's that?

S: Trying to see where they are at.

T: Why do you say that?

S: They're crawling all over the paper.

T: That's right, they are, aren't they? Hershel, what is your worm doing?

S: He's wiggling.

T: Very good. Are all your worms moving?

S: (Several students say yes.)

T: Very good, now I have some questions I want to ask you and I know you will be able to answer them.

How do you move? (pause) Diana, how do you move from place to place?

S: I walk.

T: You walk.

S: Sometimes I skip.

T: Joan, do you walk?

S: I walk mostly.

T: What parts of your body do you move? Hershel, what parts of your body do you move when you walk?

S: Your arms.

T: Anything else?

S: Your legs.

T: Anything else?

S: Toes, your feet.

S: You move your whole body.

S: How does the worm move?

S: He doesn't have any feet.

T: Are you sure?

S: I don't see any feet.

T: What is the answer to Joan's question then? Be careful of your worms.

S: By wiggling forward.

T: What do you mean, Asher?

S: He kind'a skootches along.

T: Yes. We walk and worms wiggle. Let's see how many different ways we can

Commentary

T. asks for similarities within their population of worms.

T. begins refining learning set—describing worms' movements.

T. reinforces answer involving movement.

T. tries to build S. confidence in their capabilities.

T. asks S. to transfer descriptions of movement to other animate objects.

S. asks about differences in modes of movement.

Learning set—describing different modes of movement—is established. T. pre-

Dialogue	*Commentary*
think of that animals move. How many other ways do things move besides walking and wiggling?	sents S. with problem—classifying modes of movement.

Tenth Grade World History

T: Today we are going to talk about the history of Central America. I want you all to pretend that instead of being 20th century people you are living in 600 A.D. (pause) Do you feel like you're in 600 A.D. right now? Now, you have just come to Central America. You have been migrating all this time from North America, mostly the southwestern United States and Mexico, but, of course, you didn't call them that then. How did you live before you came to Central America?

S: We must be Indians.

T: Why do you say that?

S: Because only Indians lived in North America at that time.

T: Very good. How do you think the Indians lived then?

S: Probably pretty much as they did when the white men discovered them.

T: Why is that? Remember you're talking about a span of about 1000 years.

S: *Everything* was slow before TV. (laughter)

T: Okay, you've entered a region for the first time where there is lots of rain during certain periods and the climate at other times is very dry and very hot. It's always pretty hot though because you're very close to the equator. What are some of the first things you would do?

S: Build shelter.

S: Get food.

S: Find out if there are any other people around.

T. establishes general topic.

T. begins building lifelike situation.

T. checks to see if S. possess information prerequisite to an ability to solve the problem.

T. is either satisfied that S. have necessary knowledge or has sensed the beginnings of impatience.

Dialogue *Commentary*

T: (silence) Well, that sounds like a good
start. Which should we do first?
S: Find food.
T: Do you all agree (pause)? How do you   T. presents S. with one of several prob-
do it?   lems they have identified.

Task Two Objectives

1. You should be able to teach a lesson segment eight minutes in length.
2. You should be able to select a problem appropriate to the developmental status of your students. Appropriateness of the problem will be judged on the basis of its relevance to the students and how well the entering behavior of the students fulfills the prerequisites of the problem.
3. You should be able to perform a task analysis on the problem you have selected. Your understanding of the task will be judged sufficient when your students indicate they possess behaviors prerequisite to the problems being presented.
4. You should be able to identify, through questioning or some other appropriate means, the prerequisite capabilities that are not a part of the entering behavior of your students.
5. You should be able to teach those prerequisite capabilities that are not a part of the entering behavior of your students. Adequacy will be judged by each of your students in terms of his conception of his ability to solve the problem after expending a reasonable amount of time and energy.
6. You should be able to present the problem in a manner appropriate to the arousal of an optimal level of curiosity in your students. The criterion for evaluation will be each student's estimate of the curiosity the incongruity arouses in him.

TASK TWO EVALUATION GUIDE: *WHAT?* ENCOUNTERING INCONGRUITY [2]

Teacher's Name _____

Your Name _____   *Degree of Fulfillment*

Objectives (Circle degree of fulfillment for each)	Optimal	Adequate	Minimal	Unfulfilled	Not Applic.
1. Time limit was observed within reasonable limits.	4	3	2	1	*
2. Problem was appropriate to students' developmental status.	4	3	2	1	*
3. Task analysis was sufficiently thorough.	4	3	2	1	*
4. Your missing prerequisite behaviors were identified.	4	3	2	1	*
5. Your missing prerequisite behaviors were taught (learned).	4	3	2	1	*
6. Presentation of the problem aroused your curiosity.	4	3	2	1	*

On a separate page, identify the areas in which this teacher is strong and weak. Give your suggestions for improvement. In writing your comments, remember to (a) be specific, (b) be constructive, and (c) write as extensively as you can.

[2] This form may be reproduced in limited quantities without prior permission for nonprofit instructional purposes.

Task Two Viewing/Listening Guide [3]
For Teach and Reteach Phase

Name _____

This guide is designed to assist you in structuring your tape viewing/listening so that this feedback component of the teaching laboratory will be of maximum benefit to you. Please complete and return this form to your instructor before you teach your next microlesson.

	Tallies	Total
1. Make a mark each time a student is *able* to answer a question you ask.		
2. Make a mark each time a student is *unable* to answer a question you ask.		
3. Make a mark each time a student asks you for further information.		
4. Make a mark each time you reinforce a student's contribution.		
5. Make a mark each time you do not reinforce a student's contribution.		
6. Make a mark each time you use some distracting mannerism (e.g., "uh," overuse of a specific word or phrase, etc.).		

In terms of the above information and that which you received on your comment sheets, what aspects of your teaching do you see a need to improve? How do you intend to attack these problems? How would you have taught this microlesson differently if this had been a "real" teaching situation? Write your comments on a separate page.

[3] This form may be reproduced in limited quantities without prior permission for nonprofit instructional purposes.

8

TASK THREE
So What?
Coping with Incongruity

Once Task Two's requirements have been satisfied, your students are ready, hopefully eager, to engage in problem-solving activity. Task Three requires that you consider the second phase of the problem-solving sequence, the formulation and verification of hypotheses. A natural consequent activity is trying to determine the efficacy of the guess (i.e., verifying the correct hypothesis). Advantages accrue when problem-solving becomes a group rather than an individual endeavor. Group problem-solving presupposes a group process in which individuals feel free to suggest many explanations/solutions, at times in rapid-fire succession. Such group activity is called brainstorming.

An important factor affecting brainstorming activity is the nature of the solution(s) being sought. Some problems have "right" answers while others have only "more appropriate" ones. "Appropriate" answer problems encourage divergent thinking. Students may be asked to flood the information network with possible answers as quickly as they pop into their heads. Thus, this approach fosters *low* levels of internal evaluation. "Right" answer problems require a more thoughtful approach. Students are asked to consider their contributions carefully before offering them to the group to better insure that the contributions promote the group's convergence on the solution. Thus, this approach fosters *high* levels of internal evaluation. A variation of one of these two approaches to brainstorming will most likely be appropriate for your particular topic.

Low Internal Evaluation Situations

To repeat, for highly creative, divergent situations where there are no "right" answers, where your prime interest is in reducing convergent thinking and conventionality, an appropriate approach is to encourage students to suggest possible solutions as quickly as they occur to them. Quantity is emphasized with little or no concern given to quality. Topics fitting this description would include:

> *Example:* How many different ways to use a brick can you think of?
> *Example:* If you found yourself in this situation, what are some things you might try to use to get out of it?
> *Example:* Now that you have a good knowledge of the characteristics of metal sculpture, what are some moods, themes, or ideas that seem appropriate for the medium?

The rationale upon which this approach is based is that as more and more different ideas are suggested by the group, individuals are led to look at the problem from new frames of reference. These, in turn, produce yet more unique contributions. In a sense, the process becomes cyclical and synergistic in that old ideas continually generate new and better ones.

Research supports this rationale. Parnes (1961) and Parnes and Meadow (1959) found that low internal evaluation behavior yielded a greater quantity of hypotheses, and that the hypotheses were, on the average, higher in quality than those obtained in a non-brainstorming situation. In addition, the quality of the hypotheses formulated was highest in the last half of the brainstorming session.

Three teaching strategies (or roles) are implied by these findings. When using a low internal evaluation approach, you must first obviously reduce the amount of *internal* evaluation being made by students. Removing inhibitions might be another way of describing this strategy. Internal evaluation can be reduced through pre-brainstorming instructions that encourage this kind of behavior by directing students to postpone any evaluation of the efficacy of their various suggestions until a large pool of tentative hypotheses has been established.

Second, you must be highly supportive and reinforcing to maintain the low-risk environment necessary for high student involvement. Bellack, et al. (1966) describe instruction as a game in which the teacher sets the rules of play and has the right to change them at any time. Students quickly learn that the real rules of the game implied by a teacher's *actions* and *reactions* sometimes contradict the rules he has set previously. Avoid rejecting answers as being silly or irrelevant if you have said previously that *any* idea is acceptable. In general, be sure that your actions are consistent with your instructions.

Since the quality of hypotheses increases with time, it is also important to encourage persistence. Thomas Edison once remarked that the creative process involves a great deal more perspiration than inspiration. Your task is to keep ideas flowing by using the exhortations, prompts, and hints that are a part of guided discovery.

High Internal Evaluation Situations

To repeat, many problems have "right" answers. Such problems would include:

> *Example:* What do you think caused the flame to go out?
> *Example:* How would you go about developing a formula for the problem? Let's do it step by step.
> *Example:* What kinds of effects would the introduction of the steel-headed axe have on an island culture such as this one?

In such cases, there is an advantage in having students attack a problem more directly. This goal can in part be accomplished by encouraging students to consider the efficacy of a hypothesis before offering it to the group. Guilford (1968) maintains that this sort of active evaluation is useful in situations where low-quality answers produce an interference network that is detrimental to high-quality answers but not to those of low quality. In such cases, your students need to evaluate their contributions carefully before making them.

The three teaching strategies suggested for fostering low levels of internal evaluation have equal importance here, though their application alters to fit the requirements of high internal evaluation situations. Structuring the amount of internal evaluation desired is a necessary first step. Determining the desired level requires a judgment on your part based on the nature of the problem you have selected. Setting the ground rules for the search might be another way of describing the use of this strategy in a high internal evaluation situation.

Support and positive reinforcement are also important here, but you may wish to alter your use of them. By personally avoiding substantive evaluations of contributions, you can force this task upon your students. Support and positive reinforcement thus become more a case of acknowledging and valuing the act of contributing rather than the content of the contribution. If you wish to make substantive evaluations, you can still do so in a positive manner. A flat "no" response to a student's contribution is seldom necessary even in a situation having right answers. Questioning or probing a student further can usually bring *him* to see the fallacy in his contribution, thus allowing *him* to supply the "no." This approach is still consistent with your desire to have students become more critical of their own contributions as well as those of others.

Encouraging persistence is also very important. With one exception— the use of silence—this strategy may be approached in much the same manner as it is in the low internal evaluation situations. When students are expected to be critical of their contributions, they need to be allowed time for thinking. When students are silent because they are apparently taking time to consider the situation carefully, exhortations to contribute are inappropriate. Any silence of more than a few seconds duration will undoubtedly make you feel uneasy. You will probably feel a strong urge to say something just to fill the gap in the conversation. Remember though that silence has much the same effect upon your students. Silence, when used appropriately, can be a powerful strategy for both allowing students time to think and as another method of eliciting responses from them. Exhortations, prompts, and hints are, of course, still in order whenever you judge your students' silence to be the result of a lack of ideas. Attempt to get the students to develop several alternative hypotheses. The availability of attractive alternatives will add interest to their subsequent verification procedures.

Verifying Hypotheses

At this point, your students hopefully have at hand several possible explanations for the incongruity or solutions for the problem they have encountered. The next step is for them to verify the correct or best hypothesis. In such a situation, a useful teaching strategy may be to *not* teach. Staying out of the discussion as much as possible allows students to make their own mistakes and find their own solutions.

The point during the microlesson at which the correct or best hypothesis is verified, seems to make little difference. The climax should probably come shortly before the end and you may wish to guide the verification process toward this outcome by having students work with some of the "incorrect" hypotheses first. There is, however, nothing wrong with verifying the correct or most appropriate hypothesis at the outset. If one alternative is clearly more feasible than the others, students may view a delay in verification of it as a phony attempt to avoid the obvious. Early verification of the correct hypothesis is advisable under such circumstances. Your students can then examine the other hypotheses to determine why they are unacceptable or less appropriate.

Verification procedures are usually best dictated by the nature of your subject area as well as the topic of your microlesson. One reason for teaching for process (problem-solving) objectives is to get students to think like scientists, mathematicians, linguists, artists, historians, etc. Encourage students to use the methodology of your subject area. Too little attention to process has been characteristic of the teaching of most subjects even at the undergraduate level. You may therefore be uncertain of what your discipline's methodology encompasses. Your teaching laboratory instructor can be of assistance in this case.

Stating the Principle

Another of your objectives for this microlesson is to help your students make a formal statement of the principle that reconciles the incongruity or solves the problem. Besides providing effective closure for your microlesson, having your students state the principle requires them to pull together any loose ends that may still be dangling. The activity also becomes a very effective summary since it is provided by your students. Having them state the principle is also important because it is yet another way for you *and* your students to check their comprehension of it.

The Teaching Task

If you did not take Task Two any further than the statement of the problem, this task can easily build on it. You may wish to begin by spending a minute or two reviewing the ground covered in your last microlesson. If the topic you use in this task is new, you will need to use your introductory remarks to present the new problem. Because of time limitations, assume that entering behavior has been assessed and missing prerequisites have been taught. After you have set the ground rules for the search, have students suggest hypotheses. Use those teaching strategies appropriate for helping your students collect hypotheses for the topic at hand. If it appears as though the "correct" hypothesis will not be suggested, attempt to elicit it through prompts, hints, and direct questions. Once a reasonable number of hypotheses have been formulated, move your students into the verifying phase. When the verification requirements of the task have been satisfied, have your students compose a formal statement of the principle involved to insure that they have clearly understood and assimilated it. Accomplishment of these steps satisfies the requirements for this task and you may bring your microlesson to a close.

Example Microlessons
Fifth Grade Social Studies and Science

Dialogue	*Commentary*
(T. reviews work the class has been doing with ancient civilizations and then starts describing the mystery surrounding the huge stone structures at Stonehenge, England. T. describes the general kinds of tools with which the people of Stonehenge had to work and presents the problem.)	T. sets constraints (ground rules for the search).
T: You are the people of Stonehenge. Using only simple tools, how would you go about erecting two pillars and placing a huge stone across their tops?	
S: Now, what do we have to do? I don't understand.	
T: You need to build an arch that is going to look like this (illustrates, using three wooden blocks on pile of sand), except you can't lift the stones up like this because you have nothing to lift them up with. You have no cranes or tractors or other machinery. You do have something resembling a shovel, and an axe, and probably a knife.	T. tries to clarify task. T. uses concrete objects to aid concept acquisition and simulate reality.
S: How are we going to do it then?	
T: That's the problem. How are you going to go about building your arch? (pause) Mary?	T. prompts S.
S: Get a horse.	
T: What would you do with him?	
S: A horse is stronger than I am.	
S: You might lift up the stone with a lot of horses.	
S: If you tied it on the horses, they could.	
T: How could you lift it?	T. tries to get S. to more accurately verbalize their intent.
S: Well, if you tied something around the stone, then rode the horses the other way, then it would lift it up in the air.	
T: (silence)	

Dialogue	*Commentary*
S: It would just drag.	
T: (silence) Tim thinks it would just drag. Why don't you try to show him how you would do it, Mary? Here's some string. You can pretend that it's rope and show us.	T. encourages S. to illustrate what she is having trouble verbalizing.
S: Well, if you tie it on here (pause). Well, if I tied it there and had the horses pull that way, it would go like that (illustrates by stopping base of pillar from sliding on sand and gradually raising the tied upper end with the lateral force of the horses).	
T: That's definitely one possibility isn't it? Are there any others? What if you didn't have any horses? Or what if you didn't have any rope? Janice, you look like you've got an idea.	T. reinforces contribution and calls for additional hypotheses. T. sets additional constraints.
S: Well, I just thought if you had something, you know, to keep the bottom pulled up somehow but I just don't know how to go about that. I thought if you got something underneath it and you tried to pull it up.	
T: What might you do if you get something underneath it? How might you lift it a little bit at a time? Let's see you do it—go ahead. Get some help from the other students.	T. gives S. cues. T. prompts S.
S: What about if you lifted it up a little bit and you put something underneath it?	
T: Alright, what would you lift it with?	T. asks for principle to be incorporated.
S: How about a lever?	S. identified principle.
T: Why don't you try that?	T. avoids verifying hypothesis, and asks S. to do it.
S: Well, you've got to have something else down here that will go up like that.	
T: Yes, okay. Let's assume you do. You can put a small stone there to act as a fulcrum. Now what do you do? You're holding it up along with a lot of other men.	
S: And somebody could put sand underneath there.	

Dialogue	*Commentary*
T: Let's do it. That was heavy, wasn't it, Janice?	T. tries to humorously increase reality of task.
S: Yeah. Couldn't you just keep doing that and keep lifting it up a little bit at a time?	
T: Let's try that; workers, go at it (pause). Okay, it's leaning there. Can we keep going now? Can we raise it up a little more? Eventually we would get it standing there like that. That's definitely another possibility.	T. reinforces contribution.
S: We could keep doing that for the pillars but what about the ones that go across the top?	S. identifies next step in problem.
T: That's an excellent question. Let's assume we now have both pillars standing. How do we get the third stone on top of them? It's called a "lintel", incidently.	
S: (After several aborted suggestions) You could push all the dirt up to the top and then pull it up.	S. discard their own hypotheses after wondering them out loud.
T: Can you show us what you mean, Sue?	
S: We have to make the hill steep so we could pull it up?	
T: Oh, you would make a hill? Where?	
S: All around the pillars—cover them up.	
S: Yeah and then have a whole bunch of men drag it up on top and put it on the other two stands.	
T: Fine, do it (S. illustrate procedure). Now what do you do?	
S: You would have to move all the dirt out.	
T: Go ahead.	
S: Would you do it like this?	
T: They could have, couldn't they? Which of the two ways we've worked with seems most likely to be the way that Stonehenge man built his arches?	T. avoids personally verifying hypothesis, but asks S. to do it.
S: The second.	
T: Why?	
S: Because the first takes more things—ropes and horses.	
S: You can't build the top that way anyway, so why use it at all?	

Dialogue	*Commentary*
T: Anyone think differently? (pause) Let's test our conclusion a little further. Now, if you can move the stones from somewhere else to here, can you do everything else?	
S: We just did, didn't we?	
T: Did you?	
S: Yes.	
T: I think you're right. Can anyone identify how we increased our power so that we could build our arch?	T. asks for formal statement of principles used.
S: The lever?	
T: What do you mean?	
S: We used a lever to lift up the heavy stone a little at a time.	
T: How else did we make our job easier?	
S: The sand. We piled sand under the stone after we lifted it.	
T: The sand stopped it from coming right back down while we moved the lever didn't it? (silence)	
S: We used the sand to build the hill, too.	
T: Was the hill important?	
S: It allowed us to inch the stone up on top.	
T: We used this same principle once before. Can anyone remember what it was called?	

Eleventh Grade Journalism

Dialogue	*Commentary*
T: If you will remember, last time we talked about headlines for newspapers. I gave you two stories; one was about Santa Claus. Well today I've put some heads for the Santa Claus story on the board and I'd like you all to read them and figure out which ones are good, which ones are bad (pause).	T. reviews last lesson. Heads are, in effect, hypotheses. T. presents problem and sets ground rules for the search.
S: Well, the first one says that it is a free class and this will be good because anybody will read something that has "free" written in front of it, and it says that it is offered for Santas.	
S: It's a short heading so it will probably be acceptable for that reason, because	

Dialogue	*Commentary*

you don't want a headline so long that nobody will read it.

T: Good, Sarah. How about the others?

S: The second one does not say very much.

T: Okay.

S: I think it's too short in that it doesn't give enough information in it. The first one has five words and it says an awful lot more than the second one which has three words.

T: Do you all agree with Bill (pause)?

S: The third one's too long—much too long for the small space you have.

T: Good point. Do you notice any mistakes in the third one? Anything wrong?   T. gives cue to S.

S: What's that word?

T: It's supposed to be "alias." Well, how about this word here?

S: "Perspective?" That's the wrong word; it should be "prospective."

S: Also, "course" is misspelled.

T: It obviously has a lot of problems. What about this fourth one? Gary?

S: Well, it's kinda long, too.

T: What do the rest of you think?   T. tries to involve other S.

S: I think "free" is good, but it should be more to the front where they would see it first, not sorta like an afterthought.

T: Alright, now what about this one here: "Santa School Opens." Is this head good or bad?

S: Well, it's good in a way, but yet, it doesn't say that it is free. It doesn't draw your attention as much as some of the others. "Opens" is just kinda a passive word, kinda unexciting.

T: Is that why it isn't as attention-getting, Sally?

S: Yes, . . . I guess so.

T: Alright, how about this last one? Patty, can you read it?

S: I'm not sure I can. Is that "YMCA to Establish School for Kris Kringles?"

T: Do you think that it is good or bad? What about this (points to "Kris Kringles")?

Dialogue	Commentary
S: "Kris Kringle" is cute. It's a European name for Santa Claus.	
S: It sounds like it is a little more poetic than Santa Claus but "to Establish" doesn't do very much for it—*I* don't think.	
T: Well, we've looked at all these heads; you thought some of them were good and some bad. On what are you basing your opinion? What did you look for in each one of these heads as you were going along? What would you consider to be the most important thing?	T. asks S. to identify principle(s) they have been using to judge the heads.
S: Well, I think I'd look for something catchy. It ought to be short and catchy.	
S: It should tell us something about what the story is about. It should have enough information so you'll know what you are going to read.	
T: When you are writing a head, what are you looking for? What do you want to hit the reader with?	T. asks for a more precise identification.
S: Information.	
S: Some outstanding points, too.	
S: Key words.	
T: What do you mean by key words, Bill?	
S: Ones in the story that if you look at these words you can almost figure out what the story is about. The most important ones.	
T: What do you think the key elements in our Santa Clause story are?	
S: The tuition is free.	
T: Why do you think the free tuition is the most important element? Why should you play that element up?	
S: Because this is what is going to get people to read this story and pay attention to it. They are coming to school.	
T: Alright. What are you all trying to say? Can anyone wrap this up and tie it into a nice neat package?	T. asks S. to state the principle.
S: A head should identify the key news element in a story?	

Dialogue	Commentary
T: Right, it should indicate what the important news element is. What else? Is there anything else you might look for? Or do you think that this is the *most* important thing? What can you all agree on? Is the most important consideration in writing a head the complete news value of a story?	T. avoids closure by giving S. opportunity to reconsider their conclusion.
S: I believe so. I believe it should be worded in a way that it gets your attention like "Santa Claus to School" doesn't say very much.	
T: I agree. Since you all seem to feel that the news value is most important, which one of these heads gets that point over to your readers best?	T. asks students to identify "correct" hypothesis.
S: "Free Course for Santa" (others concur).	
T: No dissenters? (pause) Very good. For next time, I'd like you to look over the other story, the one about the golden idol and come up with several heads for it—looking for the news value, the key words in the story. Pick out the ones you like best and explain why all the others you've written are weaker than it.	T. continues to encourage critical thinking by avoiding closure that might be premature. T. asks S. to apply principle in new situation.

Task Three Objectives

1. You should be able to teach a lesson segment eight minutes in length.
2. You should be able to introduce this microlesson either by concisely reviewing the previous lesson and restating the problem, or by presenting a new problem. These introductory remarks should not take more than the first minute or two of the microlesson.
3. You should be able to set adequately the ground rules for the search for hypotheses. Your instructions should be appropriate to the nature of the topic. Both criteria will be considered achieved if your subsequent actions are consistent with your instructions.
4. You should be able to be supportive and positively reinforcing of students' contributions, and correspondingly avoid negative affect.
5. You should be able to make appropriate use of silence in your microlesson. Appropriateness will be considered satisfied when time is allowed for thinking whenever a need for such time is the *apparent* cause of silence.
6. You should be able to encourage your students to be persistent through

the use of appropriate means such as exhortations, prompts, and hints whenever necessary. A necessity will be defined as an extended duration of silence that is apparently not the result of taking time to think.

7. You should be able to engage your students in using the investigative methodology (ways of thinking) of your subject area. The time available is acknowledged to be a serious limitation to the achievement of this objective and will be considered in judging its attainment.

8. You should be able to guide your students' verification procedures in an indirect manner, allowing students to largely control the procedure. Time constraints make this a difficult objective to fulfill.

9. You should be able to help your students compose a formal statement of the principle explaining the incongruity or solving the problem.

TASK THREE EVALUATION GUIDE: *SO WHAT?* COPING WITH INCONGRUITY [1]

Teacher's Name _____

Your Name _____   *Degree of Fulfillment*

Objectives (Circle degree of fulfillment for each)	Optimal	Adequate	Minimal	Unfulfilled	Not Applic.
1. Time limit was observed within reasonable limits.	4	3	2	1	*
2. Introductory statements were appropriate and concise.	4	3	2	1	*
3. Teaching behavior was consistent with stated ground rules.	4	3	2	1	*
4. Positive reinforcement was appropriately used.	4	3	2	1	*
5. Strategy of silence was used whenever appropriate.	4	3	2	1	*
6. Persistence was encouraged whenever necessary.	4	3	2	1	*
7. Discipline's investigative methodology was encouraged.	4	3	2	1	*
8. Students largely controlled the verification procedure.	4	3	2	1	*
9. Students composed a formal statement of the principle.	4	3	2	1	*

On a separate page, identify the areas in which this teacher is strong and weak. Give your suggestions for improvement. In writing your comments, remember to (a) be specific, (b) be constructive, and (c) write as extensively as you can.

[1] This form may be reproduced in limited quantities without prior permission for nonprofit instructional purposes.

Task Three Viewing/Listening Guide [2]
For Teach and Reteach Phase

Name _____

This guide is designed to assist you in structuring your tape viewing/listening so that this feedback component of the teaching laboratory will be of maximum benefit to you. Complete and return this form to your instructor before you teach your next microlesson.

	Tallies	Total
1. Make a mark for each student who actively participates in the lesson.		
2. Make a mark each time a student formulates a hypothesis (i.e., makes a guess or suggests a possible solution).		
3. Make a mark each time you reinforce a student's contribution.		
4. Make a mark each time you do not reinforce a student's contribution.		
5. Make a mark for each hypothesis for which some verification is attempted.		
6. Make a mark each time a student suggests a procedure for verifying a hypothesis or in some manner indicates that he feels he has at least partial control over the direction of the lesson.		
7. Make a mark each time it is evident that your students are thinking as persons in your discipline would think (i.e., using the investigative methodology of your discipline).		
8. Make a mark each time it is necessary for you to give direction or redirection to your students' verification process.		

In terms of the above information and that which you received on your comment sheets, what aspects of your teaching do you see a need to improve? How do you intend to attack these problems? Write your comments on a separate page.

2 This form may be reproduced in limited quantities without prior permission for nonprofit instructional purposes.

9

TASK FOUR
Now What?
Reconciling Incongruity

Your task on this microlesson requires that you accomplish two basic objectives. The first involves assessing how much your students have learned. Traditional testing procedures are only one, often quite inappropriate, method of accomplishing this goal. This fact is especially true as you attempt to engage your students in lifelike situations. Your second objective is to help your students become more conscious of the processes they have been using to solve the problem by having them verbally introspect those processes.

Two Kinds of Transfer

The third and final (*Now what?*) phase of the problem-solving process may be viewed as yet another type of verification procedure. After your students have transformed the incongruity or lifelike problem into relevant patterns of meaning, they are ready to act on the information gained by attempting to reapply or transfer it to other situations. Their questions become, "Does it work here?"; "Do I want to try any new patterns of behavior as a result of what I've learned?"; "Now what?" Often an individual is not completely confident that he has mastered a learning situation until he has proven to himself that he can apply what he has learned (the generalizable principle) in new situations. In situations where a student does not feel he needs this mastery, checking for transfer is, nevertheless, a crucial instructional strategy for assessing learning.

The learning of principles is only one of the major objectives teaching through problem-solving seeks to attain. A second is, of course, the acquisition of the process abilities, both the general problem-solving procedures and the more specialized ways of thinking (i.e., the heuristics or investigative techniques) of your discipline. The first step in this acquisition was to help your students, perhaps unconsciously, to use your discipline's investigative methodology, to have them cope with incongruity or solve a problem using the concepts that are a part of that organized body of knowledge. If students are to make significant strides toward gaining a meaningful command of your discipline, you need to make certain that they also are consciously aware of the processes or heuristics (thinking tools) they have been using as one way of better insuring their ability (power) to use these tools again (Berman, 1968). This second kind of transfer is important if you hope to develop independent students. Here, the relevant questions become "How did I do that?"; "Which actions that I took were productive?"; "Which were not?"; "What blind alleys did I explore?"; "Why?"; "How can I find the solution more easily the next time?" Encouraging your students to consider such questions helps them prepare to solve future, similar problems in a more purposeful, systematic, and confident manner.

Transferring the principle. In solving their problem, your students have probably been concerned with an isolated instance in which the principle you wish them to acquire operates. However, the true test of their command of the principle is their ability to apply it to new, and in some respects, dissimilar situations to which it generalizes. In other words, checking for transfer is an important step in assessing whether or not your students have accomplished their objective—transforming the principle into relevant patterns of meaning and thereby acquiring it.

Several means are available for accomplishing this assessment. Perhaps the most obvious is to present your students with new situations and have them explain how or why the principle applies. A second possibility is to confront your students with a situation where the principle appears to apply but in fact does not. Such an exercise helps them define the limits of the generalization with which they are working. The explanation of how or why is a good deal more demanding here and may be useful only in cases where your students thoroughly understand the principle that does explain this new situation. A third way is to have your students identify new situations in which the principle operates. Again, explanations of how and why are helpful in assuring that all your students understand the generalization.

Transferring the process. Asking your students to introspect their problem-solving activity facilitates a second kind of transfer, the difference being that the concern here is in the transference of ways of thinking (processes) rather than principles or generalizations (products). A problem-solving approach is ludicrous if your students only acquire the principle they seek. As mentioned earlier, simply telling them the principle is a great deal more efficient. The value of the problem-solving approach lies in its ability to also allow your students to experience and thereby learn from this process. Through such experience they begin to acquire the tools necessary to extend knowledge beyond its present limits.

In much the same sense that a carpenter cannot use a tool he does not own, your students cannot use a process unless they are aware of it. Admittedly, awareness of a process does not assure an ability to use it anymore than ownership of a set of tools makes one a carpenter. It is, however, an essential first step. Awareness can be gained by simply having your students talk through the procedures they have followed in arriving at a formal identification of the solution principle. You can aid this recapitulation considerably through the questions you ask your students. Why did the students formulate the hypotheses they did rather than others? How did they formulate them? Why did they choose to evaluate *that* hypothesis first? How did they verify the hypotheses? Why that method rather than this? In other words, try to lead your students to verbalize the crucial procedures they have, perhaps, unconsciously used. Introspection also gives you an opportunity to show your students how sophisticated their thinking really is. Presenting them with such evidence is a valuable way to build their confidence in their own competence.

The Teaching Task

You may find a restatement of the principle and some minor review of the last microlesson an effective opening for this one. An assessment of learning through checking for principle transfer seems a logical next step. Use whatever means you deem most appropriate for accomplishing this objective. Remember that a formal testing situation will likely stifle whatever realism you have succeeded in instilling in the previous problem-solving activity.

Once you are satisfied that your students have command of the principle, introspection is in order. Decide what the most pertinent procedures used by your students were, and plan your questioning to elicit them. Praise is important, but students should also be made aware of their mistakes so that they may avoid them in subsequent, similar situations. Remember also that a secondary goal of this microlesson is to increase your students' concept of their own competence. Assume a supportive role that will facilitate the attainment of this objective.

Example Microlessons
Sixth Grade Social Studies

Dialogue	*Commentary*
(T. has reviewed the previous lesson in which S. worked through a hypothetical situation in which they were stranded on the moon, 200 miles from their mother ship, with their life-support systems intact. Their problem involved establishing priority rankings for fifteen items available to aid them in making the trip back to the mother ship. The S. have each made their own ordering and also reached agreement as a group on a rank ordering of the fifteen items.	The fifteen items are matches, food concentrate, a rope, parachute silk, a portable heating unit, two pistols, dehydrated milk, two oxygen tanks, a stellar map, a life raft, a magnetic compass, water, signal flares, a first-aid kit, and a solar powered FM receiver-transmitter.
They have been given the "correct" ordering and the rationale for it established by a group of NASA astronauts which was confronted with the same problem.)	"Correct" hypothesis is verified.
T: Today, I'd rather not talk about *why* you made your decisions, but *how*. First of all, how was agreement reached within the group? How did the group make decisions?	T. calls for introspection of the decision-making process.
S: It seemed like the person who was called on sorta led for that question. They led the idea. You could just sorta follow it through; someone would suggest something and it would lead everybody that way.	

Dialogue	*Commentary*
T: Who became leader?	T. builds specific question from general description offered by S.
S: Mike did.	
S: He had the paper. (the original unordered list of items).	
S: What would have happened if the paper would have been switched around every so often?	
T: Is that why you permitted Mike to assume leadership? Because he had the paper? How come leadership is decided on that?	T. probes to refocus attention on the dynamics of leadership.
S: Well, he acted as narrator, so we kinda—you know . . .	S. apparently means "moderator."
S: Because he volunteered for it. That was good enough.	
T: How did the group handle situations in which there was disagreement over the importance of a particular item?	T. moves to a related point without completely developing the concept of leadership roles.
S: We talked it over until the very last minute and then we voted on it.	
T: What happened to the minority on each vote? Did you listen to that minority?	T. hints at a new direction for the discussion by asking a leading question.
S: Yeah, we did.	
S: I think we did.	
S: Most of them changed their mind.	
T: Sherry, how did you feel when you were about the only one who disagreed—I forget which item it was? Did you have any reaction when you were overruled on it several times? You were very quiet. Did you have something to say?	T. continues to focus on the behavior of specific individuals.
S: Which one? I forget. Oh, the first-aid kit maybe. You mean mad? No, because I liked everyone's ideas. I don't know very much about any of this stuff.	S. expresses feelings about herself.
T: You value other opinions more than your own, so you went along?	T. responds to S. expression of feelings.
S: Well, a part of the time anyway.	
T: Did you notice that when you were trying to make decisions—and I really thought this was neat—how you relied on someone giving information? For	T. reinforces a valuable group strategy.

Dialogue	*Commentary*
example, Ben, you provided Mike with some information for one critical decision on which he changed his mind. Didn't he? I forget which one, but it was one of them concerned with the rope—no—the pistols.	T. again focuses on individual's behavior.
S: That's right.	
T: It might be interesting to match the list you each made individually with the group's list. Do you see any patterns? which list is more accurate?	T. collects data to use in summarizing lesson.
S: Well, the group was better than me.	
T: What about you?	
S: The group.	
T: What about you?	
S: Group.	
T: And you?	
S: It was pretty close.	
T: Alright, let's focus in on this. What are you all saying?	T. asks for statement of principle.
S: Our group decision was more accurate than our individual ones, I guess.	
T: Right. That supports some of the ideas we've talked about before. Good listening, good communicating and good working together in a group will usually result in better decisions than individual members of the group can make alone. Your total knowledge was greater than that of any individual.	T. summarizes conclusions and begins working for closure.
Incidentally, if Mike hadn't assumed leadership, someone else would have. A leader was needed to get the ball rolling so that you could pool your resources, and you all unconsciously knew that (pause). Okay, good job.	T. returns to leadership concept.
Let's take a look at how our government operates and see how many places we can identify where group decisions are valued.	T. asks students to apply principle to new situations.
S: Voting's one.	
S: The House of Representatives is a group that decides things.	
S: The Senators are too.	
S: Could you call the Supreme Court one?	

Dialogue	*Commentary*

T: Could you?

S: Yes.

T: How about at the state level?

S: Same things, right?

T: What do you mean, Gary?

S: The Senate and House of Representatives and courts and all that stuff.

T: How about in our city (silence)? There are several newspapers over there. Perhaps we can find stories about groups making decisions in our town in them.

Tenth Grade Biology

Dialogue	*Commentary*

(The class has been discussing evolution and T. introduces the concept of vestigial organs. T. has asked S. to draw a picture of how each thinks man will look in a half-million years. S. have finished pictures and made some informal comparisons with those of their classmates.)

> Each picture is, in effect, the statement of a hypothesis.

T: Are there many similarities in your pictures?

S: Not much.

T: There are a couple of ways we might handle this productively. One would be to try to figure out which picture seems the most plausible. After seeing your pictures, a second thought occurred to me though and it centers on the question of *why* you think man will look the way you've drawn him. In other words, what concepts, principles, and values are you individually trying to display in your pictures? Which way shall we go?

> T. suggests veryifying hypotheses.

> T. suggests introspecting process.

S: The second: it sounds most interesting.

S: Yeah (general agreement voiced by S.).

T: Maybe we can do both at once. Ellen, you've drawn what appears to be a strongman type. Why?

Dialogue	*Commentary*
S: I don't know—I guess I think man will continue to get better and better.	
T: "Better" is an interesting word to use in this context. Better in comparison to what?	T. begins refining S. evaluative strategies.
S: To what he is now.	
S: Yeah, but the idea of adaptation means he's got to get better by definition.	
T: Do you see what Cecil's saying? (pause) Anyone?	T. tries to establish inadequacy of value judgments.
S: Do you mean that man's got to change to cope with his changing environment and that may mean changing in ways we might not consider "better?"	
T: Good point. How many of you would ask a person looking like the one you've drawn out on a date? (pause) Not many. This guy's pretty alien to us. Gary, your's has next to no legs. Why?	
S: Well, we walk a lot less now than we used to—we're more sedentary.	
T: Why will that affect our legs?	
S: Well, I guess it relates to that vestigiality we talked about.	S. applies principle.
T: Okay. Chris has got a very tall man.	
S: Because of nutrition. I was at the museum the other day and the knight's armor looks like it was made for thirteen-year-old boys.	
T: Sounds like your extrapolating—extending trends—to me. We've been getting taller and you think we might continue that. Gary, were you using the same idea in yours?	T. identifies concept and relates to previous S. contribution.
S: Yes.	
T: Here's an interesting one—very large brain cavity, small limbs, no hair, rather sickly looking. You seem to see a lot in store for us, Dave.	
S: I call 'em like I see 'em. (laughter)	
T: Why do you see us evolving this way?	
S: We're going to have to store more information; we're going to have less time to exercise or get outdoors; we're going to be a mess (more laughter).	

Dialogue	Commentary
T: How does your picture fit into all this?	
S: Well, the functions we'll have to perform will decide the direction we go.	S. identifies concept.
T: Alright. If I interpret Mary Ann's picture correctly, hers is the most ominous prediction here. Why did you leave your paper blank?	
S: I don't think man will exist in half a million years. He'll kill himself off before then.	
T: That's a very believable hypothesis—too believable for me. We're running short on time—no pun intended; which picture seems most accurate?	T. begins procedure of verifying "correct" hypothesis.
S: It's got to be between Dave's and Mary Ann's. (general agreement).	
T: Let's leave it right there. You pick the one you like depending on how optimistic your view of the world situation is. Okay? There really isn't a right answer. Can any of you think of examples of vestigial organs—parts of our body that no longer perform any useful function? (silence.)	T. asks S. to transfer principle to new situations.
S: Our appendix.	
S: Tonsils . . . and adenoids (pause).	
T: Yes. Any others?	
S: How about wisdom teeth?	
T: What do the rest of you think?	
S: We don't need 'em.	
T: Well that's a good start. There happen to be dozens. Here's a list you might find interesting (pause). How many of you feel you would draw a different man if you had it to do over? If you did, what kinds of mistakes would you avoid making? In what ways did we go wrong?	T. calls for introspection of hypothesizing process.
S: I'm not so sure we can count on what's happening now lasting that long. I don't think thinking in terms of "more of the same" will work.	
S: I just happened to think that no one added any new parts to the body. Isn't that a possibility?	

Dialogue	*Commentary*
T: We probably should have considered it, if we didn't.	
S: I had trouble mixing my values up with science, but I still have trouble thinking of us anyway other than the way we are now.	
T: Your self-condemnation is a bit too strong, Ellen. It's more a matter of just avoiding judging things too harshly from our own frame of reference.	T. tries to support S.
S: No one has really considered how the environment might change us, have they? You know . . . if it keeps getting noisier maybe our ears will get smaller and stuff like that.	
T: That's right. That really conjurs up a whole new realm of possibilities, too. So much so, that it might pay us to think about our pictures more thoroughly than we were able to today. Why don't you each try to draw a second picture for tomorrow after you hash out the problem for yourself. I've gotten some ideas for a picture from these that I'd like to try out on you.	T. begins working for some kind of closure. T. decides further "trial and error" will be productive. T. attempts to create additional interest.

Task Four Objectives

1. You should be able to teach a lesson segment eight minutes in length.
2. You should be able to make a concise review of the previous lesson.
3. You should be able to assess your students' learning by checking their ability to transfer the principle to new situations.
4. You should be able to check for transfer by using means appropriate to your topic and discipline.
5. You should be able to lead your students to introspect verbally the problem-solving act. This objective will be deemed satisfied if your students feel they are aware of the procedures they have used.
6. You should be able to foster competence by assuming a supportive role. This objective will be deemed satisfied if your students feel more capable of dealing with problems in that discipline as a result of their experience.

TASK FOUR EVALUATION GUIDE: *NOW WHAT?* RECONCILING INCONGRUITY [1]

Teacher's Name _____

Your Name _____   *Degree of Fulfillment*

Objectives (Circle degree of fulfillment for each)	Optimal	Adequate	Minimal	Unfulfilled	*Not* *Applic.*
1. Time limit was observed within reasonable limits.	4	3	2	1	*
2. A concise review of previous lesson was made.	4	3	2	1	*
3. Learning was assessed by checking for transfer.	4	3	2	1	*
4. Transfer was checked by means appropriate to the topic.	4	3	2	1	*
5. Students introspected the problem-solving process.	4	3	2	1	*
6. The lesson increased *your* conception of your competence.	4	3	2	1	*

On a separate page, identify the areas in which this teacher is strong and weak. Give your suggestions for improvement. In writing your comments, remember to (a) be specific, (b) be constructive, and (c) write as extensively as you can.

[1] This form may be reproduced in limited quantities without prior permission for nonprofit instructional purposes.

Task Four Viewing/Listening Guide [2]
For Teach Phase

Name _____

This guide is designed to assist you in structuring your tape viewing/listening so that this feedback component of the teaching laboratory will be of maximum benefit to you. Complete and return this form to your instructor before you teach your next microlesson.

	Tallies	**Total**
1. Make a mark each time a student displays an ability to transfer the principle to a new situation.		
2. Make a mark each time you encourage students to transfer the principle.		
3. Make a mark each time you reinforce a student's contribution.		

4. How well were your students able to verbalize (introspect) the learning process they had experienced?

_____

_____

_____

5. Give examples of behavior your students displayed which you consider to be evidence supporting your answer to question four.

A _____

B _____

C _____

In terms of the above information and that which you received on your comment sheets, what aspects of your teaching do you see a need to improve? How do you intend to attack these problems? Write your comments on a separate page.

[2] This form may be reproduced in limited quantities without prior permission for nonprofit instructional purposes.

Task Four Viewing/Listening Guide [3]
For Reteach Phase

Name _____

This guide is designed to assist you in structuring your tape viewing/listening so that this feedback component of the teaching laboratory will be of maximum benefit to you. Complete and return this form to your instructor before you teach your next microlesson.

	Tallies	Total
1. Make a mark each time a student displays an ability to transfer the principle to a new situation.		
2. Make a mark each time you encourage students to transfer the principle.		
3. Make a mark each time you reinforce a student's contribution.		

4. How well were your students able to verbalize (introspect) the learning process they had experienced?

_____

_____

_____

5. Give examples of behavior your students displayed which you consider to be evidence supporting your answer to question four.

A _____

B _____

C _____

This has probably been your first attempt at teaching for process objectives and your success to this point should therefore be viewed in relation to your abilities before this attempt. In effect, you too have been involved in problem-solving behavior in attempting to teach Tasks Two, Three, and Four and it may now be of some value for you to introspect the processes you have used. How many of them were intuitive? How can you make intuitive processes more purposive? Enumerate your successes, however modest you may feel they are. More importantly, identify those areas in which you feel you must improve and prescribe means you see helpful in achieving that improvement. Write your comments on a separate page.

[3] This form may be reproduced in limited quantities without prior permission for nonprofit instructional purposes.

3

Affective Concerns

10

Affect as Content

The word "affect" is commonly thought of as a verb (e.g., something affects you); but "affect" is also a noun denoting that generic amalgam of feelings, emotions, and desires that resides in each of us. The degree to which affect determines a person's overt behavior varies greatly. At times, affective concerns may be at such low levels that they have no discernible impact on behavior. At other times, affective concerns may be so strong that the behavior they stimulate overpowers all efforts at self-control.

A teacher deals with affect in two general ways. First, he maintains an ongoing attitude of support, positive regard, and personal concern for his students. His actions say to them, "You are important to me; you are more to me than a homework doer or a test taker." Secondly, the teacher is not reluctant to discuss his students' affective concerns whenever they assume dominance of their thought and behavioral processes; in such cases, the teacher allows affect to become the subject matter (content) of the lesson.

Working with affect as content requires a commitment to a long established though seldom operationalized ordering of priorities that subordinates the acquisition of knowledge and the development of skills to the discussion of affective concerns whenever the latter become a dominant influence on classroom activity. The major purpose of this chapter is to encourage, perhaps exhort, you to acknowledge the need for a personal commitment to affective concerns. Beyond commitment lies action. A teacher obviously must also have both the skills to carry out his commitment when and where affect burgeons and the sensitivity to recognize positive or negative affect when it lies, barely submerged, in the undercurrent of ongoing classroom activity.

Part III of this manual is designed to help you develop affective teaching skills by providing you with a set of teaching laboratory activities through which you can begin or, more accurately, continue acquiring the skills and sensitivity that teachers need in order to work with affect as content. The arguments presented in this chapter describe the *effective* teacher as an *affective* teacher. If these arguments have any validity, the first purpose (getting you to value affect) must be achieved or attempts to accomplish the second (helping you develop affective skills) are futile.

Affective Teaching Versus Schooling

Commitment to affective concerns implies that, at times, a teacher must, in a sense, not teach. To better understand this point, consider that affect is responsive and, therefore, relatively spontaneous; in fact, it may be more useful for you to think of it as caught, not taught. To "catch" affect, a teacher must be facilitative rather than initiative, supportive rather than evaluative, introspective rather than defensive. One might, in fact, summarize the personal characteristics of the affective teacher as being much the same set required of the teacher who values process approaches.

Over and above the personal qualities required to operate in the affective domain, the affective teacher must circumvent the constraints of the institutional process that has come to be known as schooling. "Schooling" has become a dirty word that connotes a set of operational definitions of the teaching-learning process that effectively, if unintentionally, mute affect in schools. Specifically, schooling is dysfunctional to affective concerns because of the way it operationally defines (i.e., deduced from how most schools actually operate) teaching (as information-giving), learning (as information-collecting), the teacher-student relationship (as businesslike, impersonal, and task-oriented), and legitimate subject matter (as that factual knowledge with which students' parents feel comfortable). Silberman (1970, p. 10) summarizes schooling's impact on students.

> "The most deadly of all possible sins," Erik Erikson suggests, "is the muti-
> lation of a child's spirit." It is not possible to spend any prolonged period
> visiting public school classrooms without being appalled by the mutilation
> visible everywhere—mutilation of spontaneity, of joy in learning, of pleas-
> ure in creating, of sense of self. The public schools—those "killers of the
> dream," to appropriate a phrase of Lillian Smith's—are the kind of insti-
> tution one cannot really dislike until one gets to know them well. Be-
> cause adults take the schools so much for granted, they fail to appreciate
> what grim, joyless places most American schools are, how oppressive and
> petty are the rules by which they are governed, how intellectually sterile
> and esthetically barren the atmosphere, what an appalling lack of civility
> obtains on the part of teachers and principals, what contempt they un-
> consciously display for children as children.

It goes without saying that one must not confuse stated definitions with practiced ones, for in schools the disparity between the two can be gross.

How It Can Be

Schooling's definitions need not be accepted. Alternatives exist. As a teacher, you can help your students become more complete, fully func-tioning, self-actualizing individuals. You can replace the schools' near total attention to cognition and skill development with a regimen that includes healthy portions of loving and humaneness by allowing students the freedom to build on success rather than flee from failure. You can pay more than lip service to human dignity by respecting human rights.

What we become is a product of how we behave; becoming is, in a sense, habitual behaving. How each of us behaves is a product of how we perceive our world (Combs, 1962). If schools are uncivil to students, they will perceive it, and in turn, behave as people normally do in the face of discourtesy and impoliteness; they will, in like, behave in an uncivil manner. If the behavior is both widespread and persistent, it becomes habit. Uncivility becomes a normal mode of behavior for our society and its members become uncivil human beings. (Perhaps we already have.)

You can take significant steps toward turning this trend around by implementing alternative definitions of teaching, learning, the teacher-student relationship, and what should be learned that will permit affect to become an integral part of the curriculum.

Teaching.   Rogers (1969, pp. 103–4) sketches in an alternate definition of teaching as he erases the present one.

. . . Teaching, in my estimation, is a vastly over-rated function.

Having made such a statement, I scurry to the dictionary to see if I really mean what I say. Teaching means "to instruct." Personally I am not much interested in instructing another in what he should know or think. "To impart knowledge or skill." My reaction is, why not be more efficient, using a book or programmed learning? "To make to know." Here my hackles rise. I have no wish to *make* anyone know something. "To show, guide, direct." As I see it, too many people have been shown, guided, directed. So I come to the conclusion that I do mean what I said. Teaching is, for me, a relatively unimportant and vastly overvalued activity.

But there is more in my attitude than this. I have a negative reaction to teaching. Why? I think it is because it raises all the wrong questions. As soon as we focus on teaching the question arises, what shall we teach? What, from our superior vantage point, does the other person need to know? I wonder if, in this modern world, we are justified in the presumption that we are wise about the future and the young are foolish. Are we *really* sure as to what they should know? Then there is the ridiculous question of coverage. What shall the course cover? This notion of coverage is based on the assumption that what is taught is what is learned; what is presented is what is assimilated. I know of no assumption so obviously untrue. One does not need research to provide evidence that this is false. One needs only to talk with a few students.

Learning and the teacher-student relationship.   Rogers' outline for the affective teacher, as well as more desirable definitions of learning and the teacher-student relationship become clearer as one examines the impact of contemporary society on the concept of education. Increasing pressures for social change accompany accelerating technological change. Mead (1969) believes society and culture are now changing so rapidly that the amount of the culture possessed by the old that will be of any use to the young is diminishing rapidly. The concept of education as the vertical transmission of culture from the old to the young is moribund if not already dead. The older generation possesses progressively less of the expertise needed by the young to survive in contemporary society and the young are becoming aware of it.

Because the needs of the young are increasingly incompatible with the expertise of the old, the authority of expertise upon which schools have traditionally relied is losing its power as an agent of order. Schools have also relied heavily on the authority of rules, many of which are little more than arbitrary dicta. They too are being challenged and consequently have lost much of their effect as an agent of order.

Benne (1970) sees the need to establish order in contemporary educational contexts around a third type of authority, one that he calls anthropogogical authority. The order emanating from anthropogogical authority is based on the contemporary need of all persons to continually re-educate themselves in order to keep pace with a rapidly evolving society.

Teacher and student roles lose definition as two or more people engage in mutual explorations of the unknown, each applying his own particular expertise to the problems at hand. A colleague relationship of mutual support and respect develops, and out of this colleagiality, order arises.

Legitimate subject matter. The colleague relationship requires that notions of what constitutes legitimate subject matter be markedly altered. It implies that students have as much to say about what will be learned as teachers do. Since the quality of the teacher-student relationship affects what will be learned, it too becomes content. Learning acquires the personal meaning it needs to become permanent. In large part, the student becomes the content; his feelings, motives, aspirations, and values become valid subject matter as the learning process forces them into his and his teacher's consciousness.

For affect to become content, a teacher must take advantage of those situations in which feelings and emotions, both his and his students', become prime concerns. As a teacher, you must provide information that will help your students achieve a better understanding of their own feelings. You must continually strive to improve human relationships in your classroom (Frymier, 1969). Under such circumstances, education becomes personal growth. Teaching becomes helping a student go where *he* has to go. Discipline becomes helping students constructively vent their feelings, emotions, and desires rather than forcing them to subdue all perceptible clues suggesting that affect even exists.

Affective Microteaching Tasks

The ensuing chapters of this manual describe four affective tasks, each focusing on one dimension of the human relationship. Each task has its own central objective.

"Empathizing" requires you to get to know your students at the affective level, to come to understand what they are feeling, why they are feeling that way, and what you and they can do to find more appropriate ways of dealing with those feelings. One might describe the central question you need to answer as, *"Who are you?"* The task requires you to begin finding out what makes your students tick.

"Respecting" requires you to assume that a student is capable of constructive action and act accordingly, even when "instinct" may tell you to do otherwise. The task requires you to take steps toward establishing Benne's notion of colleagiality by initiating supportive behavior. Here, the central question becomes, *"Who are we?"*

"Being Genuine" requires you to stop hiding behind the teaching role, to take off your teaching mask and become a real person. For two people to establish a helping relationship, they must first establish mutual trust. When your emotions, feelings, and desires are withheld from students, an important part of you remains unknown to them; you remain a role. People cannot trust roles; they can only trust other people. The "Being Genuine" task requires you to be a person in a teaching context. In this task, the central question becomes, *"Who am I?"*

"Communicating Concretely" requires that you help your students avoid the kind of vague, oblique, and evasive statements that inhibit the development of strong relationships and the analysis of feelings. An integral requirement of the task is that you too must communicate in concrete, specific terminology when discussing feelings. The central question to be answered on this task becomes *"What are we saying?"*

A perplexing paradox will develop as you attempt to use the teaching strategies imbedded in these four tasks, and it may well explain why affect is so poorly attended to in our schools. Affect is most difficult for a teacher to confront, let alone cope with constructively when the situation in which it occurs is most traumatic and threatening, and it is exactly under such harsh circumstances that it becomes most important to do so. Empathizing at such times may well open a Pandora's box of hostile feelings; respecting may result in your being personally rebuffed and hurt; being genuine may make you look foolish and insecure at a time when you most crave respect, integrity, and security; helping students communicate their feelings in concrete terms may be asking them to say precisely those things that you do not want to confront even in vague abstractions. None of these situations is likely to occur. Rather, you are more likely to experience the power that affective approaches have to turn complacency, anxiety, or hostility in positive directions as well as increase the productivity of the warm, enjoyable events that occur in your classroom.

One might say that this chapter asks you to use uncommon sense. It asks you to be fully human by not being a "teacher." Coping with affect requires you to act when the natural response is to react. Using affect as content implies that you can be mindful of the consequences of your actions. Affective approaches require that you be secure enough in your own humanity to lay your humaneness on the line when it is most threatened. Maintaining a joyful classroom requires that you allow joy to enter it.

11

Role-Playing for Affect[1]

The previous chapter briefly described four teaching tasks that contain teaching strategies which will enable you to deal with feelings (affect) aroused in you and your students. The tasks are "Empathizing" (understanding the feelings of your students); "Respecting" (maintaining positive regard for your students); "Being Genuine" (facilitating person-to-person interaction by avoiding hiding behind the teacher role); and "Communicating Concretely" (helping your students discuss personally relevant material in specific and concrete terminology). Each of these tasks requires you to respond to a spontaneous incident or problem, the nature of which you will have no prior knowledge. Producing such an incident becomes an additional role-playing responsibility of your students.

[1] This chapter may be skipped if you will be teaching to real students rather than role-playing peers. In that case, however, the children and/or adolescents acting as students should either read the chapter or receive instruction on the information it contains.

Example Incidents

The following is a list of some example incidents that have worked well for each of these tasks. Note that many incidents, though identified with a specific task, will work for other tasks as well. The list is far from exhaustive and should be expanded to include many incidents appropriate to the teaching situations which you and your colleagues are most interested in exploring.

Incidents Appropriate for the "Empathizing" Task

Grade Level	*Behavior*
K–2	One student goes and stands by the teacher. When asked what's wrong or to sit down, he holds the teacher's hand and starts to cry. He has a reason.
K–6	One student interrupts the teacher to tell him something remote from the lesson: "My daddy . . ." He is persistent.
1–9	One student asks to leave the room. He leaves whether he has permission or not. He returns shortly. In a moment, he asks to leave again, etc. He has a reason.
4–12	One student becomes increasingly inattentive. He moves from subtle behaviors (blank stare, doodling) to more obvious behaviors (staring out the window, laying his head down). He does not respond the first time the teacher calls on him. The second time he is questioned, he accuses the teacher of picking on him. ("I wasn't doing anything!") His problem is very personal.
6–12	One student appears despondent and withdrawn. He has a personal problem and when asked, "What's wrong?" is reluctant to discuss it. If pushed, he becomes hostile.
7–12	One student intently reads a book from the very start of the microlesson. He has a big test in a hard subject next period and must study for it. Grades are very important to him. He responds to the teacher accordingly.
8–12	About two minutes into the microlesson, one student asks, "Just once, why can't we discuss something we're interested in?"
9–12	One student draws a picture. His only interest is art.

Incidents Appropriate for the "Respecting" Task

Grade Level	*Behavior*
K–4	One student asks an irrelevant question within the same subject area but on an entirely different topic. He is persistent.
K–6	One student plays with some object (e.g., a pencil as an imaginary airplane). He is persistent.
2–7	Two students have a shoving match. They start with nudges and escalate activity.
4–7	One student pulls the hair of another of the opposite sex. He tries to do it on the sly at first but becomes increasingly bold.
4–8	One student writes a note that reads, "Read this, giggle, and pass it on" and begins passing it.
4–12	One student is quite restless. When asked about it, he picks up some introductory term the teacher has used and says he doesn't understand it. He is very slow and does not catch on.
5–12	One student becomes increasingly distracted until the teacher makes a concerted effort to get him involved in the microlesson.
6–12	Two students whisper and laugh. They continue until the teacher *effectively* intervenes.
7–12	One student is the class clown. He does his best to keep the students laughing.
8–12	One student does some personal grooming (e.g., combing hair or applying makeup). He has not heard a word.
8–12	Several students ask one at a time to go to the restroom. When the teacher balks at the continuing parade, the refused student becomes irate. ("I *really* have to go! I'm not like all those goof-offs!") He is serious about it.

Incidents Appropriate for the "Being Genuine" Task

Grade Level	*Behavior*
K–3	One student interrupts the teacher with some personal question like "Do you kiss your boyfriend?" He is persistent.
2–6	One student draws a very uncomplimentary picture of the teacher and labels it with his name. He passes it around the class. Other students may embellish the original drawing.

Grade Level	*Behavior*
4–9	One student has an abundance of nervous energy. He beats out rhythms on the desk, taps his feet, etc. When the teacher asks him to stop, he tries to, but he just cannot. In a minute or so he is back at it.
4–12	One student drops his books accidentally. Others pick up the idea and begin doing it on purpose.
7–12	One student tries to take over the class by talking. He has answers or questions for everything. He tries to move the discussion in new directions, etc.
8–12	About one minute into the microlesson one student starts making sarcastic comments about the lesson to the student(s) next to him. He is not particularly concerned about whether or not the teacher hears him. He knocks the lesson in any way he can. When confronted by the teacher, he responds in this frame of mind.
8–12	One student is very angry. He slams things around. When asked about it, he responds with hostility to the teacher as a person. He holds the teacher in very low esteem and is not afraid to tell him so.
9–12	One student is a know-it-all. He has a cocky attitude. ("I dare you to teach me, help me, do anything for me. You think you're such a good teacher, try to teach *me* something.")

Incidents Appropriate for the "Communicating Concretely" Task

Grade Level	*Behavior*
K–1	One student is frightened of something and starts crying. He wants his mother.
K–6	One student is very withdrawn and unresponsive. When called on, he remains silent. If the teacher persists, he tells the teacher he doesn't like him. He has a reason.
2–6	One student is upset. Another teacher has criticized him harshly and unfairly on the playground at recess. His anger becomes more and more obvious until the teacher responds to it.
3–8	One student feels the animosity toward the opposite sex that is typical of this age group ("Girls/boys are for the birds."). An opposite sexed student has done something to offend him and he decides to retaliate by making remarks about the student during class.
4–10	One student pushes another's books off his desk. The second student complains and demands retribution.
8–11	One student is beside himself with joy. He has just heard that he has been elected president of an important school organization. He can scarcely contain his emotions and his attention is completely removed from the lesson.

Grade Level	*Behavior*
11–12	One student is fed up. He is "sick and tired of all the meaningless game-playing" that school requires of him. Shortly into the lesson, the teacher does something that becomes the straw that breaks the camel's back. The student explodes.
12	At the end of his previous class, one student has received back an exam which he has failed badly. A good grade in the course was crucial to his college plans. He is despondent and withdrawn.

Procedure for Generating an Incident

A method must be devised for generating appropriate affective incidents for each teacher's microlesson. Individual situations will require individualized procedures for generating incidents, but some variation of the following method will probably work for most.

Prior to his microlesson, the teacher announces the grade level he will be teaching. A student or the teaching laboratory instructor selects an incident appropriate for that grade level. Those listed in this chapter may be used or additional incidents may be constructed for this purpose. Each incident is written on a card. The selected incident card is mixed with several blank cards which are then distributed to the students. The blank cards insure that the teacher cannot prematurely focus his attention on the "problem" student. Only the student receiving the incident card initiates the action described. Once the teacher begins dealing with the problem, students with blank cards may support the teacher or the student executing the incident or they may sit quietly. The class should definitely avoid a circus of activity since extreme disorder is very difficult to cope with within the constraints of the teaching laboratory. In general, the students should respond to the situation in what they feel is a natural way, at all times trying to be as realistic a group of students for their teacher as they can. Remember that your goal is not to try to psychologically annihilate him—though, at times, a teacher's reaction to an incident suggests such a response. Rather, your goal is to give your teacher a setting in which he can develop those skills that will allow him to strengthen his interpersonal relationships with his students.

12

TASK FIVE
Who Are You?
Empathizing

This microteaching task describes teaching strategies which hope-fully will enable you to attend to your students' feelings, particularly those that may be detrimental to the effective functioning of your class and/or individual students. Teachers and students are continually acting and reacting on the basis of their feelings. Despite this fact, the accepted rules of the teaching-learning game generally preclude players from at-tending to the unexpressed feelings that are motivating students' ob-servable behavior. The following situation may illustrate this point.

Example: A teacher of an above average class has trouble maintaining class-wide discussions, because they are invariably dominated by three intelligent, verbally aggressive students. Although they have said nothing, most of the other members of the class are visibly upset by the talkative triumvirate. The teacher is aware of the problem and has attempted to redirect the discussion to other members, but to no avail. The combina-tion of their growing animosity and the continuing domination of the discussion by the three students has had its effect; the class remains reticent.

This teacher is aware of the feelings present in his room, which places him one step ahead of many, but subtle attempts to change the situation are having little success. He may be reluctant to deal directly with the problem because three well-meaning students may be badly hurt in the process. He may also be aware that the problem is getting worse and that to continue to avoid the issue may build an even higher wall around the three. For the moment, he has chosen not to expose their humaneness by empathizing with the rest of the class. The feelings present in this classroom are impeding teaching and learning; they are preventing *human* interaction. Failure to acknowledge students' feelings has turned teacher and student into roles and teaching and learning into a game—a game, in this example, that the teacher is losing. Note, however, that the situation is just as tragic when feelings are not acknowledged and the teacher is winning.

The point is that you would be wise to consider your students' feelings valid subject matter whenever you judge those feelings to be inhibiting group interaction or individual learning. The conviction required to accomplish this task involves far more than the simple inclination that it is important to initiate an occasional, idle discussion about feelings whenever the pressure to cover content is for some reason reduced. Rather, accomplishment of the task requires an ongoing attitude on your part and subsequently on the part of your students that establishes a priority on dealing with feelings and group process whenever they are affecting the course of human events in your classroom. The group process jargon refers to such activity as "dealing with the here-and-now." Attending to the here-and-now by examining students' feelings is an important step in building the foundation upon which individual integrity, mutual respect, and discipline (in the original sense of the word) can be established.

Empathy

This task focuses on one very important dimension of human interaction—empathy. Empathizing is the act of imaginatively projecting one's own consciousness into another person. To empathize is to try to perceive a situation as another does and to understand why that person feels as he does. The act of teaching may be viewed as an act of helping of which empathy is a key ingredient.

Carkhuff (1969a, pp. 174–5; 1969b, pp. 315–17) identifies five levels of empathic understanding. The first four levels of this scale comprise a useful construct for viewing the modes of behavior a teacher may use in dealing with students' feelings. They are, excepting the examples,[1] produced almost verbatim here.[2]

Level 1.   Level one represents the lowest possible level of interpersonal functioning. At this level, the verbal and behavioral expressions of the teacher either *do not attend to or detract significantly from* the verbal and behavioral expressions of the student in that they communicate significantly less of the student's feelings and experiences than the student has communicated himself. In other words, the teacher communicates no awareness of even the most obvious, expressed, surface feelings of the student. The teacher may be disinterested in the student or simply operating from a preconceived frame of reference (such as his lesson plan or an inaccurate expectation level) which totally excludes that of the student.

Example:
S: Why can't we talk about something interesting for a change?
T: (Either ignores S. comment or says) Your parents don't pay me to conduct a "fun and games" class; they pay me to teach you history and that's what I intend to do.

Example:
S: The same bunch of kids gets to do *everything* around here.
T: (Either ignores S. comment or says) If you'd complain less and work harder, you could be involved in a lot of activities, too.

In summary, the teacher does everything but express that he is listening, understanding, or being sensitive to even the most obvious feelings of the student in such a way as to detract significantly from the communications of the student. Level one expressions are often negative and/or of such a nature as to arouse negative (hostile) feelings in students.

Level 2.   At this level, the teacher responds to the expressed feelings

---

[1] Since it is often useful to think of affect as being caught, not taught, the examples presented in this part of the manual will be presented in a different manner from the example microlessons in the process part of the manual. Examples presented in each affective teaching task attempt to portray spontaneous events that might well occur within the context of any lesson. To aid you in discriminating between levels and to highlight the relative effectiveness of each, the same incidents are used for all four levels of a given task.

[2] An important alteration made not only in this scale, but also those adapted for the ensuing three tasks is the respective substitutions of "teacher" and "student" for Carkhuff's "first person" and "second person." Obviously, teachers and students are not alone in sharing the relationships described in the four scales used in this part of the manual. Counselor and counselee, parent and child, minister and layman—in short, human and human—can all benefit from the concepts imbedded in these scales.

of the student, but he does so in a manner that *subtracts noticeable affect* from the communications of the student. In other words, the teacher may communicate some awareness of obvious, surface feelings of the student, but his communications drain off a level of the affect and *distort the level of meaning.* The teacher may communicate his own ideas of what may be going on, but these are not congruent with the expressions of the student.

Example:
S: Why can't we talk about something interesting for a change?
T: How can you expect me to *always* make this class interesting for *all* of you? After all, you *do* have a lot of different interests. I realize that this isn't very interesting, but it's information you'll need to work subsequent problems.

Example:
S: The same bunch of kids gets to do *everything* around here.
T: Now Betty, do you really think that's true? Just look at how many students in our class are involved in various extra-curricular activities. Jim and Jerry are on the football team, Sue is a . . . (etc.).

In summary, the teacher tends to respond to something other than what the student is expressing or indicating.

Level 3. At this level, the expressions of the teacher in response to the expressions of the student are essentially interchangeable with those of the student in that they express essentially the same affect and meaning. In other words, the teacher responds with accurate understanding of the surface feelings of the student but may not respond to or may misinterpret the deeper feelings.

Example:
S: Why can't we talk about something interesting for a change?
T: I thought this would interest you. What is it about today's discussions that disinterests you?
S: Oh, I don't know. I guess it's because I've had most of this stuff before.
T: How many of the rest of you think we'd get more mileage out of a different topic? (Several hands go up). That's a significant number. Was this topic pretty well covered in earth science last year?
S: (Several say yes) Mr. Wall spent most of a six-week period on it.
T: How about those of you that had Mr. Miser? (little response) I'd say we've got a problem. Half of you seem to have had this and half haven't. Maybe we can work out a way of satisfying both groups. Any suggestions?

Example:
S: The same bunch of kids gets to do *everything* around here.

T: (pause) That's a pretty strong statement, Dave. By "around here" do you mean our class or the school in general or what?

S: The whole school's that way, this class included.

T: How is this class that way?

S: Well, for instance, you always call on the same students. About half of us are lucky to get a chance to speak even once a *week*.

T: I call on students who raise their hands—or have I been missing something?

S: Oh, forget it.

T: No, I won't forget it. This is important. It's important to you or you wouldn't have brought it up. I *know* it's important to me, and I would guess that it might be important to many of the others. Am I right? How many of you feel there are times when you'd like to make a contribution but for some reason are unable to?

In summary, the teacher is responding so as to neither subtract from nor add to the expressions of the student. He does not respond accurately to how that person really feels beneath the surface feelings; but he indicates a willingness and openness to do so. Level three constitutes the minimal level of facilitative interpersonal functioning. To be dealing at all effectively with the affect in his classroom, a teacher should be operating at least at this level.

Level 4.   Level four represents the deepest level of facilitative interpersonal functioning normally experienced in a classroom setting (a fifth level is experienced rarely in one-to-one counseling settings). At level four, the responses of the teacher add noticeably to the expressions of the student in such a way as to express feelings a level deeper than the student was able to express himself. In other words, the teacher communicates his understanding of the expressions of the student at *a level deeper than they were expressed,* and thus, enables the student to experience and/or express feelings in more abstract terms or helps the student establish why he feels as he does.

Example:

S: Why can't we talk about something interesting for a change?

T: I thought something's been bothering you, George. I'm glad you brought it out in the open. What bothers you about this lesson?

S: It's not really just this lesson, just classes in general; they're usually so—so irrelevant.

T: Do most of you find this to be true? (pause) How many of you think you have too little control of what happens to you in school? (many hands) How do you usually feel when you're forced into situations you have little control of?

S: Mad.

S: Frustrated.

S: Angry.

T: How about you, George?

S: I guess all those.

T: Me too, but why do we feel that way? (Class goes on to discuss factors that can cause anger and list constructive means through which they can make a significant input into instructional settings.)

Example:

S: The same bunch of kids gets to do *everything* around here.

T: Do you feel left out of things, Ellen?

S: Well—not me so much, but . . . well, look at the P.A. announcements this morning. Every girl that got nominated for homecoming queen was a cheerleader or a club president or something.

T: Were some of your friends pretty disappointed in the way the nominations went?

S: Yes.

T: You used the homecoming nominations as an example, but it sounds like you're talking about a much broader problem than just this one incident. Do some students feel they are systematically excluded from most school activities?

S: *I* think so.

T: How about the rest of you? (a few students express agreeement with Ellen) Let's see if we can examine how someone goes about getting involved in activities to see if we can spot some problems in the process. Where should we start?

In summary, the teacher's responses add deeper feeling and meaning to the expressions of the student.

The Teaching Task

Your task is to teach a microlesson in which you attempt to engage your students in problem-solving activity (see Part II [3]). During the lesson a preplanned, observable expression of feelings will occur (see Chapter 11). To insure spontaneity, you will have no prior knowledge of the nature of the event or of who will initiate it. The observable act might be as subtle as the distraction of one student or as obvious as a student saying he would rather talk about something more interesting.

Your task includes dealing with whatever incident occurs during your lesson. You should attempt to deal with the feelings that emerge at least at level three of the empathy scale. In other words, your expressions in response to your students' expressions of feelings should, at a minimum, be essentially interchangeable. Strive for level four but this is a difficult goal to achieve within the constraints of the teaching laboratory. Again,

[3] If you have not taught the tasks described in Part II, Chapter 5 includes examples of problem-solving microlessons. A review of that chapter may provide you with sufficient background to plan a microlesson for the *empathizing* task.

your objective is to work through the incident by dealing with the feelings that are impeding learning for your student(s). Once you have accomplished the objective to your satisfaction, you may immediately terminate your microlesson. Accomplishing the task will probably require you to forsake your planned lesson. You may be reluctant to do so, but remember that a major purpose of this part of the manual is to bring you to realize the importance of doing exactly that whenever the need arises.

Students' Roles

Role-playing students have an additional responsibility in making this task a beneficial activity for teachers since it is crucial that their roles be as believable as possible. Students should consult Chapter 11 for suggested incidents to use and procedures for employing them. These incidents are designed to arouse feelings and thus produce highly affective situations in which you and your colleagues can work on empathizing skills.

Task Five Objectives

1. You should be able to teach a lesson segment eight minutes in length.
2. You should be able to teach for some process (problem-solving) objective.
3. You should be able to identify the occurrence of an observable act displaying feelings, during the lesson (level one behavior).
4. You should be able to forgo your previous lesson plan in order to deal with the feelings displayed.
5. You should be able to discuss the feelings causing the incident with your student(s) at least at level three of the empathy scale.

TASK FIVE EVALUATION GUIDE: *WHO ARE YOU?* EMPATHIZING [4]

Teacher's Name _____

Your Name _____   *Degree of Fulfillment*

Objectives (Circle degree of fulfillment for each)	Optimal	Adequate	Minimal	Unfulfilled	Not Applic.
1. Time limit was observed within reasonable limits.	4	3	2	1	*
2. The lesson required problem-solving behavior.	4	3	2	1	*
3. The expression of feelings was identified.	4	3	2	1	*
4. Feelings were dealt with as valid subject matter.	4	3	2	1	*
5. *Lowest* level of empathic understanding achieved was		1	2	3	4
6. *Highest* level of empathic understanding achieved was		1	2	3	4

On a separate page, identify the areas in which this teacher is strong and weak. Give your suggestions for improvement. In writing your comments, remember to (a) be specific, (b) be constructive and (c) write as extensively as you can.

[4] This form may be reproduced in limited quantities without prior permission for nonprofit instructional purposes.

Task Five Viewing/Listening Guide [5]
For Teach and Reteach Phase

Name _____

This guide is designed to assist you in structuring your tape viewing/listening so that this feedback component of the teaching laboratory will be of maximum benefit to you. Complete and return this form to your instructor before you teach your next microlesson.

	Tallies	Total

1. Make a mark each time you seek information about *how* the student feels or *why* he feels that way.

2. Make a mark each time you feel you make a premature judgment about the nature of the problem.

3. How well do you think you were able to reconcile the problem?

   _____

   _____

4. Would you have handled the incident differently if you had another chance? If so, how?

   _____

   _____

5. List the kinds of evidence you have that indicate that the problem was satisfactorily reconciled.

   A _____
   B _____
   C _____
   D _____

In terms of the above information and that which you received on your comment sheets, what aspects of your teaching do you see a need to improve? How do you intend to attack these problems? Write your comments on a separate page.

[5] This form may be reproduced in limited quantities without prior permission for nonprofit instructional purposes.

13

TASK SIX
Who Are We?
Respecting

A crucial dimension of interpersonal functioning is respect. Being respected by students is a central concern of most teachers. In their efforts to obtain respect, some teachers foolishly *demand* it and get, instead, a shallow facade of acquiescence that lasts only until their backs are turned. Others attempt to *buy* respect with permissiveness or a just-one-of-the-boys stance that ultimately achieves the opposite effect.

Think for a moment about those people whom you genuinely respect. Their personalities may be quite diverse, but they all have one characteristic in common—they all respect you. To earn the respect of students a teacher must first respect them. The problem is as simple and complex as that. Respecting some students requires very little effort; you like them and respect is a natural response. However, every honest teacher admits he has students whom he dislikes. Respecting these students by accepting them as they are without attaching unnecessary reservations can be an extremely demanding, but nevertheless necessary task if you hope to teach them. Counselors refer to the task as maintaining or expressing unconditional positive regard toward students. Since you are more knowledgeable, more mature, and presumably more flexible than your students, you are expected to take the initiative in developing a respecting relationship with them.

Respect

One important way of communicating respect for students is by making obvious efforts to understand them, thereby indicating the importance you place in the values they hold and the ideas they have (Bordin, 1957). Respect is, in this sense, closely related to empathy. The latter involves an awareness of another's feelings. Respect requires that you be able to display positive regard for those feelings and additionally for the individual possessing them. Because of this relationship, differentiating empathy from respect is sometimes difficult. For the purposes of this manual, that problem need not be of great concern to you.

Respect is presented as a separate task in this manual because it can also be communicated to students in the relative absence of empathic understanding. An example of a high respect, low empathy teacher is the benevolent dictator type who consistently considers his students capable of constructive action, but has little interest in them beyond how well they are performing in his class. Nothing could be more alien to his classroom than a discussion of or reference to feelings, be they his students' or his own. Valuing students and their achievements is an important part of his conception of teacher; understanding students' feelings is not.

Respect is not always warmly expressed and may, under some circumstances, be communicated in anger. For instance, somewhere among your respected teachers there is probably at least one "whip-cracker" who succeeded in clearly communicating his awareness of your importance and potential despite his gruff teaching style. At times, anger may be a most appropriate mode for communicating concern for students. The following situation illustrates this point.

> *Example:* It is the first week of school. A student decides to test the limits of acceptable behavior with his teacher. The teacher is writing at the board as a piece of wadded paper rolls to rest near her feet. She picks it up, places it in a nearby wastebasket, and continues writing. Activity escalates—more paper. The teacher takes no action. The class is becoming boisterous; one student walks to the front of the room, picks up several pieces of paper and returns to his seat to throw them again. Teaching and learning have broken down completely in the carnival atmosphere.

The crux of the issue centers on the students' obvious awareness that their behavior is improper. The teacher's apathy toward it may be easily interpreted by them as indicating that she does not care enough about them to stop the disruption. If she does not care, why should they? Disruptive behavior should be confronted. The desired goal is to clearly communicate your awareness that the disruptive students are capable of *constructive* action as you reprimand them.

One cautionary note should be given regarding the use of anger or related expressions of feelings: be certain that you are not simply responding defensively to a situation that challenges *unearned* authority that you have considered to be "granted" anyone assuming the teaching role. Students may be trying to tell you that some aspect of the role you are playing is phony. Responding to the incident by resorting to further role-prescribed behavior (i.e., "getting on the muscle") may be the most debilitating action you could take.

Carkhuff (1969a, pp. 178–9; 1969b, pp. 317–18) identifies five levels of respect. The key criterion enabling one to discriminate between the various levels is the extent to which the teacher is open to the possibility that the student is capable of acting constructively within the context of the situation in which he finds himself. The first four levels of the scale comprise a useful construct for viewing the modes of behavior a teacher may use to communicate respect for students (or a lack of it). They are, excepting the examples, produced almost verbatim here.

Level 1. Level one represents the lowest possible level of interpersonal functioning. At this level, the verbal expressions of the teacher communicate a clear lack of respect (or negative regard) for the student. In other words, the teacher communicates to the student that the student's feelings and experiences are not worthy of consideration or that the student is not capable of acting constructively. The teacher may become the sole focus of evaluation.

Example:
S: I just don't understand how to do these problems.
T: Well, what do you expect when you don't even bother to crack the book?

Example:
S: (Has said nothing but has been squirming in his seat for some time.)
T: Steve, just for once will you sit still and try paying attention?

In summary, the teacher in many ways communicates a total lack of respect for the feelings, experiences, and potentials of the student(s). Level one expressions are often negative and/or of such a nature as to arouse negative (hostile) feelings in students.

Level 2.   At this level, the teacher responds to the student in such a way as to communicate little respect for the feelings, experiences, and potentials of the student. In other words, the teacher may respond mechanically or passively or ignore many of the feelings of the student. The teacher's responses indicate that he harbors considerable doubt that the student is capable of constructive action.

Example:
S: I just don't understand how to do these problems.
T: I know they're difficult; you'll just have to work harder.

Example:
S: (Has said nothing but has been squirming in his seat for some time.)
T: Steve, please stop that fidgeting. What on earth's going on?

In summary, the teacher in many ways displays a lack of respect or concern for the student's feelings, experiences, and potentials.

Level 3.   At this level the teacher communicates a positive respect and concern for the student's feelings, experiences, and potentials. In other words, the teacher communicates respect and concern for the student's ability to express himself and to deal constructively with the situation that is concerning him.

Example:
S: I just don't understand how to do these problems.
T: At which step in the process do you first have trouble, Sandy?

Example:
S: (Has said nothing but has been squirming in his seat for some time.)
T: Is there something wrong, Steve?

In summary, the teacher in many ways communicates that who the student is and what he does matters to the teacher. Level three constitutes the minimal level of facilitative interpersonal functioning. To be dealing effectively with the affect in his classroom, a teacher should be operating at least at this level.

Level 4.   Level four represents the deepest level of respect normally experienced in a classroom setting (a fifth level is experienced rarely in one-to-one counseling settings). At level four, the teacher clearly communicates a very deep respect and concern for the student. In other words, the teacher's responses enable the student to feel free to be himself and experience being valued as an individual. The teacher displays complete confidence in the student's ability to deal constructively with the situation that is concerning him.

Example:

S: I just don't understand how to do these problems.

T: I think I know how you feel, John. It's really frustrating to go all out on something and *still* have trouble with it. Let's go over it again and see if we can figure out where the snag is.

Example:

S: (Has said nothing but has been squirming in his seat for some time.)

T: Steve, you seem to be uncomfortable. Could you use a break?

In summary, the teacher communicates a very deep caring for the feelings, experiences, and potentials of the student.

The Teaching Task

Your task is to teach a microlesson in which you again attempt to engage your students in problem-solving activity (see Part II [1]). During the lesson a preplanned, observable incident will occur (see Chapter 11). To insure spontaneity, you will have no prior knowledge of the nature of the event or of who will initiate it. The observable act may be very subtle (e.g., the squirming student mentioned above) or quite obvious as when a student initiates a dramatic, emotional confrontation with you.

Your task includes dealing with whatever incident occurs during your lesson. You should attempt to deal with it in a manner that clearly displays your respect for the student(s) involved. In doing so, you should attempt to operate at least at level three of the respect scale. In other words, your response to the incident should, at a minimum, clearly transmit to your students that you consider them capable of constructive action. Once you have accomplished this objective to your satisfaction, you may immediately terminate your microlesson.

Students' Roles

As was the case on the empathizing task, role-playing students have an additional responsibility in making this task a beneficial activity since it is crucial that their roles be as believable as possible. Students should again consult Chapter 11 for suggested incidents to use. These incidents are designed to produce situations which tax a teacher's ability to respond in a respecting manner.

[1] If you have not taught the tasks described in Part II, Chapter 5 includes examples of problem-solving microlessons. A review of this chapter may provide you with sufficient background to plan a microlesson for the *respecting* task.

Task Six Objectives

1. You should be able to teach a lesson segment eight minutes in length.
2. You should be able to teach for some process (problem-solving) objective.
3. You should be able to identify the occurrence of an observable incident during the lesson.
4. If necessary, you should be able to forgo your previous lesson plan in order to deal with the incident.
5. You should be able to deal with the incident with your student(s) at least at level three of the respect scale.

TASK SIX EVALUATION GUIDE: *WHO ARE WE?* RESPECTING [2]

Teacher's Name _____

Your Name _____   Degree of Fulfillment

Objectives (Circle degree of fulfillment for each)	Optimal	Adequate	Minimal	Unfulfilled	Not Applic.
1. Time limit was observed within reasonable limits.	4	3	2	1	*
2. The lesson required problem-solving behavior.	4	3	2	1	*
3. The incident was identified.	4	3	2	1	*
4. Dealing with incident superseded original lesson.	4	3	2	1	*
5. *Lowest* level of respect achieved was		1	2	3	4
6. *Highest* level of respect achieved was		1	2	3	4

On a separate page, identify the areas in which this teacher is strong and weak. Give your suggestions for improvement. In writing your comments, remember to (a) be specific, (b) be constructive and (c) write as extensively as you can.

[2] This form may be reproduced in limited quantities without prior permission for nonprofit instructional purposes.

Task Six Viewing/Listening Guide [3]
For Teach and Reteach Phase

Name _____

This guide is designed to assist you in structuring your tape viewing/listening so that this feedback component of the teaching laboratory will be of maximum benefit to you. Complete and return this form to your instructor before you teach your next microlesson.

1. How well do you think you were able to reconcile the incident?

   _____
   _____
   _____

2. Would you have handled the incident differently if you had had another chance? If so, how?

   _____
   _____
   _____

3. List the statements you made which you feel are evidence that you were operating at least at level three of the respect scale.

   A _____
   B _____
   C _____
   D _____

In terms of the above information and that which you received on your comment sheets, what aspects of your teaching do you see a need to improve? How do you intend to attack these problems? Write your comments on a separate page.

[3] This form may be reproduced in limited quantities without prior permission for nonprofit instructional purposes.

14

Who Am I?
Being Genuine

To develop a close relationship with his students, a teacher must be genuine. Within the context of teaching, being genuine includes those efforts a teacher makes to transcend the teaching role—to reveal, in a sense, his humaneness. In describing some of the problems a teacher encounters as he attempts to be genuine, Greenberg (1969, pp. 25–36) identifies a number of popularly-held myths that impede a teacher's efforts to teach with feeling. Several of them constitute a useful compendium of premises a teacher must *reject* if he is to be genuine.

The myth of calmness. The teacher should behave calmly and coolly at all times.

The myth of moderation. The teacher's feelings should be subdued, especially those that are the most intense, deep, and painful.

The myth of loving all students. The teacher should like all students identically, having no dislikes for specific students or specific behavior in students.

The myth of hiding one's true feelings from students. The teacher, with effort, can stop students from knowing how he really feels.

A former student expressed the effect produced by a teacher's acceptance of such myths in this manner:

> I remember walking into a grocery store when I was in about seventh grade and seeing my teacher. I was appalled—I mean, my God, there she stood before me with slacks on (not her teaching outfit) buying food. Until that time I just never considered that she ate. [I thought] . . . she survived on chalk dust or something. Anyway that was my first realization that we were both humans and such a barrier between us really should not exist.

The general converse to Greenberg's collection of myths would go something like this. Teachers are human with human feelings, many of which are difficult or impossible to hide even from the youngest of students. Teachers are most human when they expose their humaneness by sharing their significant feelings with their students. Teachers are at their best when they are trying not to be teachers (the chalk-devouring variety) or to hide behind a role. Teachers are being most human when they are being most genuine.

Genuineness

When a teacher expresses his hurt when it hurts, when he expresses his joy when he is joyous, he is taking important but difficult first steps toward becoming genuine. When a teacher becomes a trusted friend, he has arrived.

Two basic steps are necessary to achieve genuineness. A teacher must first be honest with himself. If a teacher is not *aware* that he is being defensive, there is no way he can take corrective measures. The second step is obviously to be honest with his students. Imagining an effective teacher who has not at least achieved the first step is difficult indeed. Imagining a friend who has not achieved the second step is even more demanding.

Genuineness can also cause problems. When a potentially destructive person is genuine, the result is destructive interaction. There are people who genuinely desire to exploit, who gain solace from hurting or defaming others. To advise such a person to be as genuine as possible would undoubtedly be damaging to both him and those with whom he has contact. An appropriate course would be to advise him not to teach. Exhortations to be genuine should not be interpreted as free license to express hostility. Such actions may have cathartic or even therapeutic value for the teacher but this is obviously not one of the things schools are for. Teacher actions that have a deleterious effect on students simply have no place in the classroom. Teachers *can* express a wide range of feelings constructively; the purpose of this task is to help you do just that.

Carkhuff (1969a, pp. 184–6; 1969b, pp. 319–20) identifies five levels of genuineness. The first four levels comprise a useful construct for viewing the modes of behavior a teacher may use in dealing with his own feelings in classroom settings. They are, excepting the examples, produced almost verbatim here.

Level 1.   Level one represents the lowest level of interpersonal functioning. At this level, the teacher's verbalizations are clearly unrelated to what he is feeling at the moment, or his genuine responses are negative in regard to the student(s) and appear to have a totally destructive effect upon the student(s). In other words, the teacher may be defensive in his interaction with the student(s) and his defensiveness may be demonstrated in the content of his words or the quality of his voice. Where he is defensive, he does not employ his reaction as a basis for potentially valuable inquiry into the relationship.

Example:
S: You come on *so* strong with all that moralistic crap about good this and bad that. Well, let me tell you that it's all goin' in one ear and out the other. As far as I'm concerned, you ain't even there!
T: When I want your opinion, I'll ask for it! You've got a lot to learn *including* the fact that *no* teacher can do a good job with a lazy student.

Example:
T: Why are you doing that, Roy?
S: It really bugs you doesn't it? Well, that's why I do it—because it bugs you so much.
T: Well, you pull that stunt again and *I'll* bug *you*—right out of school!

In summary, there is evidence of considerable discrepancy between the inner experiencing of the teacher and his concurrent verbalizations. Where there is no discrepancy, the teacher's reactions are employed solely for destructive purposes.

Level 2.   At this level, the teacher's verbalizations are slightly unrelated to what he is feeling at the moment, or when his responses are genuine, they are negative in regard to the student(s). The teacher does not appear to know how to employ his negative reactions constructively as a basis for inquiry into the relationship. In other words, the teacher may respond to the student(s) in a "professional" manner that has a rehearsed quality concerning the way a teacher "should" respond in that situation.

Example:

S: You come on *so* strong with all that moralistic crap about good this and bad that. Well, let me tell you that it's all goin' in one ear and out the other. As far as I'm concerned, you ain't even there!

T: Where did you learn to talk to a teacher like that! And by the way, how many more times am I going to have to tell you that there isn't any such word as "ain't?"

Example:

T: Why are you doing that, Roy?

S: It really bugs you doesn't it? Well, that's why I do it—because it bugs you so much.

T: Roy, you'd better learn how to get along with authority figures. You're going to have real problems in life if you don't.

In summary, the teacher is usually responding according to his prescribed role rather than expressing what he personally feels or means. When he is genuine, his responses are negative, and he is unable to employ them as a basis for further inquiry.

Level 3. At this level, the teacher provides no "negative" cues between what he says and what he feels, but he provides no positive cues to indicate a really genuine response to the student(s). In other words, the teacher may listen and follow the student(s), but commits nothing more of himself. There is no apparent conflict between his verbal and nonverbal communications.

Example:

S: You come on *so* strong with all that moralistic crap about good this and bad that. Well, let me tell you that it's all goin' in one ear and out the other. As far as I'm concerned, you ain't even there!

T: Most of us have felt that way about a teacher at some time or other. I'm sorry you feel that way about me. We obviously have very different value systems.

Example:

T: Why are you doing that, Roy?

S: It really bugs you doesn't it? Well, that's why I do it—because it bugs you so much.

T: Well, you're right; it does. So I guess you win this round. Now let's stop playing games and get some work done. Okay?

In summary, the teacher appears to make appropriate responses that do not seem insincere but that do not reflect any real involvement with the student(s) either. Level three constitutes the minimal level of interpersonal functioning. To be dealing effectively with the affect in his classroom, a teacher should be operating at least at this level.

Level 4. Level four represents the deepest level of genuineness normally experienced in classroom settings (a fifth level is experienced rarely in one-to-one counseling settings). At level four, the teacher presents positive cues indicating a genuine response (whether positive or negative) in a nondestructive manner to the student(s). In other words, the teacher's expressions are congruent with his feelings, although he may be somewhat hesitant about expressing them fully.

Example:
  S: You come on *so* strong with all that moralistic crap about good this and bad that. Well, let me tell you that it's all goin' in one ear and out the other. As far as I'm concerned, you ain't even there!
  T: Obviously what you've just said bothers me, Sylvia. So much so that I'm not sure just how to respond. I guess the thing that upsets me most is that I'd really like to be someone you consider important, but I don't know what I've been doing or saying that's brought this on.

Example:
  T: Why are you doing that, Roy?
  S: It really bugs you, doesn't it? Well, that's why I do it—because it bugs you so much.
  T: That doesn't upset me half as much as the implications of what you just said. What's happened to make you feel such a strong need to retaliate? I think I just now—this very minute—realized that I don't really know who you are, Roy. (pause) What's most disastrous is that I can't remember ever really trying. I know talk's cheap but let me say that that's going to change.

In summary, the teacher responds with many of his own feelings, and there is no doubt that he really means what he says. He is able to employ his responses, whatever their emotional content, as a basis for further inquiry into the relationship.

The Teaching Task

Your task is to again teach a microlesson in which you attempt to engage your students in problem-solving activity (see Part II [1]). During

---

[1] If you have not taught the tasks described in Part II, Chapter 5 includes examples of problem-solving microlessons. A review of this chapter may provide you with sufficient background to plan a microlesson for the *being genuine* task.

the lesson a preplanned, observable incident will occur that is designed to provoke feelings in you (see Chapter 11). To insure spontaneity, you will have no prior knowledge of the event or of who will initiate it. Again, the observable act may be comparatively subtle (e.g., a student walking in and out of the room whenever he sees fit to do so) or quite obvious (e.g., the ". . . you ain't even there!" example mentioned above).

Your task includes dealing with the feelings aroused in you as a result of the incident. You should attempt to deal with your feelings at least at level three of the genuineness scale. In other words, your expressions in response to your feelings should, at a minimum, communicate no negative cues or contradictory information between what you say and how you feel. Remember that a level four response is again a desirable though unrequired goal. Once you have accomplished the task objective to your satisfaction, you may immediately terminate your microlesson. Accomplishing the task may again require you to forsake your planned lesson.

Students' Roles

Role-playing students have the same responsibilities they had on the two previous affective tasks. The same procedure for setting up incidents may be followed. Students should again consult Chapter 11 for suggested incidents to use. These incidents are designed to produce situations that will arouse many feelings in a teacher, feelings that teachers do not often feel comfortable expressing.

Task Seven Objectives

1. You should be able to teach a lesson segment eight minutes in length.
2. You should be able to teach for some process (problem-solving) objective.
3. You should be able to identify the occurrence of an observable problem incident during the lesson.
4. You should be able to forgo your previous lesson plan as long as necessary to deal with your feelings.
5. You should be able to respond to the feelings aroused in you by the incident at least at level three of the genuineness scale.

TASK SEVEN EVALUATION GUIDE: *WHO AM I?*: BEING GENUINE [2]

Teacher's Name _____

Your Name _____   Degree of Fulfillment

Objectives (Circle degree of fulfillment for each)	Optimal	Adequate	Minimal	Unfulfilled	Not Applic.
1. Time limit was observed within reasonable limits.	4	3	2	1	*
2. The lesson required problem-solving behavior.	4	3	2	1	*
3. The problem incident was identified quickly.	4	3	2	1	*
4. Dealing with the incident superseded the lesson plan.	4	3	2	1	*
5. *Lowest* level of genuineness achieved was		1	2	3	4
6. *Highest* level of genuineness achieved was		1	2	3	4

On a separate page, identify the areas in which this teacher is strong and weak. Give your suggestions for improvement. In writing your comments, remember to (a) be specific, (b) be constructive, and (c) write as extensively as you can.

[2] This form may be reproduced in limited quantities without prior permission for nonprofit instructional purposes.

Task Seven Viewing/Listening Guide [3]
For Teach and Reteach Phase

Name _____

This guide is designed to assist you in structuring your tape viewing/listening so that this feedback component of the teaching laboratory will be of maximum benefit to you. Complete and return this form to your instructor before you teach your next microlesson.

1. How well do you think you were able to reconcile the problem?

   _____

   _____

2. Would you try to communicate your feelings differently if you had another chance to do so in a similar situation? If so, give examples of the kind of expressions you would deem more appropriate.

   A _____
   B _____
   C _____

3. Identify those statements you made that you feel indicate that you satisfactorily communicated your feelings (that indicate that you were, in fact, genuine).

   Statement A _____

   _____

   Statement B _____

   _____

   Statement C _____

   _____

4. What level of genuineness were you using in each of these statements?
   Statement A: Level _____; Statement B: Level _____;
   Statement C: Level _____

5: Try to rewrite each of these statements (not presently at level four) so that it is at least one level higher than it was originally stated as a part of your microlesson.

   Statement A _____

   _____

   Statement B _____

   _____

   Statement C _____

   _____

In terms of the above information and that which you received on your comment sheets, what aspects of your teaching do you see a need to improve? How do you intend to attack these problems? Write your comments on a separate page.

[3] This form may be reproduced in limited quantities without prior permission for nonprofit instructional purposes.

15

TASK EIGHT
What Are We Saying?
Communicating Concretely

Chapter 3 (p. 17) discussed the importance of teachers clearly communicating their instructional objectives to their students. Before they can accomplish a task you have set for them, your students must understand in clear, concrete terms what the task is. This chapter discusses the importance of accurate communication within a different context—one that involves the expression of feelings.

We communicate with others in many different ways. With some people we may use a very formal, impersonal approach. We use personal referents in a very general, abstract, and often evasive manner. An example of this way of communicating is the standard greeting, "Hello, how are you?" Think of how unexpected and unwanted would be a response that *really* attempted to communicate how you feel.

Under other circumstances with other people, we are less formal and remote. Our behavior, including our way of communicating, becomes more casual and trusting as the relationship does. Remarks are less guarded as the feeling of being judged by others diminishes. The discussion of personally relevant material becomes appropriate, though the level of trust established may not be sufficient for us to make serious attempts to communicate that material with any meaningful degree of accuracy or for us to encourage others to do so.

Less frequently, we may strive with still other people to develop deeper levels of trust, honesty, and openness. We may seek or offer help to others in developing new insights into ourselves, them, or our relationship. To do so, we try to communicate even nebulous concepts (like feelings) as concretely as possible. Ideas, even fairly sensitive ones, are confronted head on; the evasions which characterize our normal verbal sparring become blatantly inappropriate.

The closeness of an interpersonal relationship and the concreteness of the language used are closely related. This relationship suggests two important ways you, as teacher, can initiate deeper interpersonal relationships with your students. First, you can strive to describe the qualities of your present relationship as precisely as possible. Second, you can help your students also to master the ability to communicate concretely both with you and with their fellow students.

Concreteness

This task focuses on how you and your students can more concretely communicate personally relevant information. It describes how you and they can begin to express ideas relating to your interpersonal relationships and your concerns about those relationships in more specific terms. In other words, this task should give you the skills to begin tearing down the wall of words behind which teachers and students so often and so comfortably hide.

Carkhuff (1969a, pp. 192–3; 1969b, pp. 323–4) identifies five levels of concreteness or specificity of expression in interpersonal processes. The first four levels of this scale comprise a useful construct for viewing the different ways of communicating personally relevant information useful both within the classroom context and in private conferences. They are, excepting the examples, produced almost verbatim here.

Level 1. Level one represents the lowest possible level of interpersonal functioning. At this level, the teacher leads or allows all discussion with the student(s) to deal only with vague and anonymous generalities. In other words, the teacher and the student(s) discuss everything on strictly an abstract and highly intellectual level.

Example:
S: You're one of the few teachers in this school who tries to understand us.

T: Come now, Mary; you know better than that. Many of the teachers in this school try to help students.

Example:
T: Is something troubling you, Jeff?
 S: (Looks at T., but does not respond)
T: Cat got your tongue?

In summary, the teacher makes no attempt to lead the discussion into the realm of personally relevant specific situations and feelings.

Level 2. At this level, the teacher frequently leads or allows even discussions of material personally relevant to the student(s) to be dealt with on a vague and abstract level. In other words, the teacher and the student(s) may discuss their "real" feelings but they do so at an abstract, intellectualized level.

Example:
 S: You're one of the few teachers in this school who tries to understand us.
T: Thank you for the compliment. Sometimes we teachers have our hands full just keeping up with you kids, let alone understanding you.

Example:
T: Is something troubling you, Jeff?
 S: (Looks at T., but does not respond)
T: I guess there are times when we'd all like to be left alone.

In summary, the teacher does not elicit discussion of most personally relevant feelings and experiences in specific and concrete terms.

Level 3. At this level, the teacher at times enables the student(s) to discuss personally relevant material in specific and concrete terminology. In other words, the teacher makes it possible for the discussion with the student(s) to center directly around most things that are personally important to the student(s), although there will continue to be areas not dealt with concretely and areas which the student does not develop fully in specificity.

Example:
 S: You're one of the few teachers in this school who tries to understand us.
T: That's great to hear. What are we doing that makes us closer together than you are with most of your other teachers?

Example:
T: Is something troubling you, Jeff?

S: (Looks at T., but does not respond)
T: Is it a problem you have trouble putting into words?

In summary, the teacher sometimes guides the discussion into consideration of personally relevant specific and concrete instances, but these are not always fully developed. Level three constitutes the minimal level of facilitative interpersonal functioning. To be dealing at all effectively with the affect in his classroom, a teacher should be operating at least at this level.

Level 4. Level four represents the most concrete level of communication normally experienced in a classroom setting (a fifth level is experienced rarely in one-to-one counseling settings). At level four, the teacher is frequently helpful in enabling the student(s) to fully develop in concrete and specific terms almost all instances of concern. In other words, the teacher is able on many occasions to guide the discussion to specific feelings and experiences of personally meaningful material.

Example:
S: You're one of the few teachers in this school who tries to understand us.
T: I really appreciate your telling me that. But what do I do that makes you feel more important than you do with most of your other teachers?

Example:
T: Is something troubling you, Jeff?
S: (Looks at T., but does not respond)
T: When I have a problem, I often find it helps to just talk about it with a friend, someone who's just a good listener. I'd like to try to be that friend for you.

In summary, the teacher is very helpful in enabling the discussion to center around specific and concrete instances of most important and personally relevant feelings and experiences.

The Teaching Task

Your task is to again teach a microlesson in which you attempt to engage your students in problem-solving activity (see Part II [1]). During the lesson a preplanned, observable expression of feelings will occur (see

---

[1] If you have not taught the tasks described in Part II, Chapter 5 includes examples of problem-solving microlessons. A review of this chapter may provide you with sufficient background to plan a microlesson for the *communicating concretely* task.

Chapter 11). To insure spontaneity, you will have no prior knowledge of the nature of the event or of who will initiate it. The observable act might range from a warm, pleasant situation such as a student complimenting you to a hostile, threatening one in which a student expresses considerable hatred toward you, a fellow student, or the school.

Your task includes dealing with whatever incident occurs during your lesson. In doing so, try to operate at least at level three of the concreteness of communication scale. In other words, you should attempt to be open to your students' discussion of personally relevant material and you should attempt to help them express their feelings about that material in specific and concrete terminology rather than vague abstractions. Strive for level four, but this is a difficult goal to achieve within the constraints of the teaching laboratory.

Again, your objective is to work through the incident by dealing with the feelings that may be impeding learning for your student(s). Using statements stripped of vague and ambiguous terminology, try to accurately identify the sentiment imbedded in your students' behavior. Try to help them perceive their situation in a more concrete and specific manner.

Once you have accomplished this objective to your satisfaction, you may immediately terminate your microlesson. Accomplishing the task will probably require that you forsake your planned lesson. You may be reluctant to do so, but remember that a major purpose of this part of the manual is to bring you to realize the importance of doing exactly that whenever the feelings present in your classroom make it difficult for your students to concentrate on their learning task.

Students' Roles

Role-playing students again have an additional responsibility in making this task a beneficial activity, since it is crucial that their roles be as believable as possible. Students should consult Chapter 11 for suggested incidents to use. The incidents are designed to produce expressions of feelings which you and your students can attempt to deal with in a concrete and specific manner.

Task Five Objectives

1. You should be able to teach a lesson segment eight minutes in length.
2. You should be able to teach for some process (problem-solving) objective.
3. You should be able to identify the occurrence of an observable expression of feelings, during the microlesson.

4. You should be able to forgo your previous lesson plan in order to deal with the expression of feelings using concrete and specific terminology.
5. You should be able to discuss the feelings causing the incident with your student(s) at least at level three of the concreteness of communication scale.

TASK EIGHT EVALUATIVE GUIDE: *WHAT ARE WE SAYING?*: COMMUNICATING CONCRETELY [2]

Teacher's Name _____

Your Name _____   *Degree of Fulfillment*

Objective (Circle degree of fulfillment for each)	Optimal	Adequate	Minimal	Unfulfilled	Not Applic.
1. Time limit was observed within reasonable limits.	4	3	2	1	*
2. The lesson required problem-solving behavior.	4	3	2	1	*
3. The expression of feelings was identified.	4	3	2	1	*
4. Feelings were dealt with as valid subject matter.	4	3	2	1	*
5. *Lowest* level of concreteness achieved was		1	2	3	4
6. *Highest* level of concreteness achieved was		1	2	3	4

On a separate page, identify the areas in which this teacher is strong and weak. Give your suggestions for improvement. In writing your comments, remember to (a) be specific, (b) be constructive and (c) write as extensively as you can.

---

[2] This form may be reproduced in limited quantities without prior permission for nonprofit instructional purposes.

Task Eight Viewing/Listening Guide [3]
For Teach Phase

Name _____

This guide is designed to assist you in structuring your tape viewing/listening so that this feedback component of the teaching laboratory will be of maximum benefit to you. Please complete and return this form to your instructor before you teach your next microlesson.

	Tallies	Total

1. Make a mark each time you attempt to help your students communicate in more concrete and specific terminology.

2. Make a mark each time you feel you succeed in getting your students to communicate in more concrete and specific terminology.

3. Write down two or three key statements you make during your microlesson in which you were consciously trying to communicate concretely.
   Statement A _____
   _____
   Statement B _____
   _____
   Statement C _____
   _____

4. What level of concreteness were you using in each of these statements?
   Statement A: Level _____; Statement B: _____;
   Statement C: Level _____

5. Try to *rewrite* each of these three statements (not presently at level four) so that it is at least one level higher than when it originally was stated as a part of your microlesson.
   Statement A _____
   _____
   Statement B _____
   _____
   Statement C _____
   _____

In terms of the above information and that which you received on your comment sheets, what aspects of your teaching do you see a need to improve? How do you intend to attack these problems? Write your comments on a separate page.

[3] This form may be reproduced in limited quantities without prior permission for nonprofit instructional purposes.

Task Eight Viewing/Listening Guide [4]
For Reteach Phase

Name _____

This guide is designed to assist you in structuring your tape viewing/listening so that this feedback component of the teaching laboratory will be of maximum benefit to you. Please complete and return this form to your instructor before you teach your next microlesson.

	Tallies	Total

1. Make a mark each time you attempt to help your students communicate in more concrete and specific terminology.

2. Make a mark each time you feel you succeed in getting your students to communicate in more concrete and specific terminology.

3. Write down two or three key statements you make during your microlesson in which you were consciously trying to communicate concretely.
   Statement A _____

   Statement B _____

   Statement C _____

4. What level of concreteness were you using in each of these statements?
   Statement A: Level _____; Statement B: Level _____;
   Statement C: Level _____

5. Try to *rewrite* each of these three statements (not presently at level four) so that it is at least one level higher than when it originally was stated as a part of your microlesson.
   Statement A _____

   Statement B _____

   Statement C _____

Tasks Five, Six, Seven, and Eight have required you to experiment with several concepts and teaching roles, some of which may have been foreign to your previous concept of teaching. How comfortable do you feel using affective teach-

---

[4] This form may be reproduced in limited quantities without prior permission for nonprofit instructional purposes.

ing strategies now that you have experienced them firsthand? Which strategies are you able to use most easily? In what areas do you most need to improve for you to be able to deal adequately with the affective concerns of your students? What are some specific steps you intend to take to achieve this improvement? Write your comments on a separate page.

4

Personal Concerns

16

TASK NINE
What Kind of Teacher Am I Now?
Culminating Microlesson

This manual has asked a lot of you. It has asked you to teach in specific ways. Some were familiar, others strange. If this manual has been successful, you have been steadily building a pool of your own ideas about teaching and yourself and about the teacher you would like to be. As you moved from task to task, you may have experienced growing frustration with the lack of opportunities to try these ideas out. This final task offers you a first opportunity to do just that. The task also marks an ending to this microteaching experience.

But endings are also beginnings. This microlesson marks the beginning of your more independent efforts to improve as a teacher, and it is perhaps your first real opportunity to show yourself and others what kind of teacher you are now. It gives you a chance to examine what you have learned, how you have changed, and how you feel about the changes that have occurred.

The Teaching Task

Your task for this microlesson is to prepare and teach an extended lesson segment that exemplifies the kind of teacher you have come to value.[1] You are not being asked to apply any or all of the teaching strategies described in this manual. Do so only if they are a part of the profile of the teacher you have come to value. Because this task's charge, like Task One's, is to be yourself, this microlesson will not be formally evaluated. This microlesson is a chance for you to take stock of where you were, where you have come, and where you are going. Have fun with it and learn something about yourself.

Checking Overall Learning

If you were able to save the recording of your first microlesson (see p. 14) you now have an opportunity to assess the degree of change that has taken place in your teaching over the span of your microteaching experience. Has there been a significant change? If so, what is the nature of the change? Are you a better teacher? In what ways? Has your microteaching experience been worth the effort you have expended on it?

Task Nine Objectives

1. You should be able to teach an extended lesson segment that exemplifies the kind of teacher you have come to value.

Task Nine Viewing/Listening Guide [2]

Name _____

This guide is designed to assist you in structuring your tape viewing/listening so that this feedback component of the teaching laboratory will be of maximum benefit to you. Please complete and return it to your instructor in the next few days.

1. If the tape of your first microlesson is still available, view (or listen to) it again. What are your general impressions of it in retrospect?

---

[1] Your teaching laboratory instructor will specify the time limit for you. Ideally, this microlesson should be at least fifteen minutes long to permit you the freedom to teach as you would like.

[2] This form may be reproduced in limited quantities without prior permission for nonprofit instructional purposes.

_____

2. What were your dominant feelings and impressions as you taught this final micro-lesson? Of what were you most aware? Have your dominant feelings and impressions about your teaching changed since your first microlesson?

_____
_____
_____
_____

3. As you view (or listen to) your tape recording, what aspects of it concern you most? Has the focus of your attention changed since your first microlesson?

_____
_____
_____

4. What are you saying a teacher is by the manner in which you taught this last micro-lesson?

_____
_____
_____

5. Try to identify three or four strengths that you have either developed or become aware of during your microteaching experience.

A _____
B _____
C _____
D _____

6. Try to identify three or four weaknesses that you most feel a need to eliminate. Also try to prescribe a specific plan of attack to eliminate each of these weaknesses. In doing so, try to avoid vague statements like, "I just need more practice at it . . ." or, "I can't do much about it until I'm actually teaching."

A _____
B _____
C _____
D _____

How has microteaching helped you most? How would you change it to make it more beneficial? Write your comments on a separate page.

Bibliography

ALLEN, DWIGHT and KEVIN RYAN. *Microteaching.* Reading, Mass.: Addison-Wesley, 1969.

AMSTER, HARRIETT. "Effect of Instructional Set and Variety of Instances on Children's Learning." *Journal of Educational Psychology* 57:74–85 (1966).

BANDURA, ALBERT and R. WALTERS. *Social Learning Through Imitation.* New York: Holt, Rinehart & Winston, 1963.

BELLACK, ARNO A., HERBERT M. KLIEBARD, RONALD T. HYMAN, and FRANK L. SMITH, JR. *The Language of the Classroom.* New York: Teachers College Press, Columbia University, 1966.

BENNE, KENNETH D. "Authority in Education." *Harvard Educational Review* 40:385–410 (1970).

BERLYNE, DANIEL E. "An Experimental Study of Human Curiosity." *British Journal of Psychology* 45:256–65 (1954).

BERMAN, LOUISE M. *New Priorities in the Curriculum.* Columbus, Ohio: Charles E. Merrill, 1968.

BESTOR, ARTHUR E. *Educational Wastelands: The Retreat from Learning in Our Schools.* Urbana: University of Illinois Press, 1953.

————. *The Restoration of Learning: A Program for Redeeming the Unfulfilled Promise of American Education.* New York: Knopf, 1955.

132

BORDIN, E. S. "Ambiguity as a Therapeutic Variable," *Journal of Consulting Psychology* 19:9–15 (1955).

BORTON, TERRY. *Reach, Touch and Teach: Student Concerns and Process Education.* New York: McGraw-Hill, 1970.

BROUDY, HARRY S. "Laboratory, Clinical, and Internship Experience in the Professional Preparation of Teachers." *Ideas Educational* 2:5–13 (1964).

BRUNER, JEROME S. *The Process of Education.* Cambridge, Mass.: Harvard University Press, 1960.

———. "The Act of Discovery." *Harvard Educational Review* 31:21–32 (1961).

CARKUFF, ROBERT R. *Helping and Human Relations: A Primer for Lay and Professional Helpers.* Vol. One. New York: Holt, Rinehart & Winston, 1969a.

———. *Helping and Human Relations: A Primer for Lay and Professional Helpers.* Vol. Two. New York: Holt, Rinehart & Winston, 1969b.

COMBS, ARTHUR W., ed. *Perceiving Behaving Becoming.* Washington, D.C.: Yearbook of the Association for Supervision and Curriculum Development, 1962.

DAVIS, O. L., JR., and THOMAS B. GREGORY. "Laboratory Components in Teacher Education or Practicing What We Preach." Center for Research and Development in Teacher Education Monograph Series, The University of Texas at Austin, 1968. Mimeographed.

———. "Laboratory Components in Teacher Education." *Peabody Journal of Education* 47:202–7 (1970).

FESTINGER, LEON. "Introduction to the Theory of Cognitive Dissonance." In *Personality: Readings in Theory and Research,* Edited by Eugene A. Southwell and Michael Merbaum, pp. 378–97. Belmont, Calif.: Wadsworth, 1964.

FRYMIER, JACK R. "Teaching the Young to Love." *Theory into Practice* 8:42–4 (1969).

FULLER, FRANCES F. "Concerns of Teachers: A Developmental Conceptualization." *American Educational Research Journal* 6:207–26 (1969).

GAGNÉ, ROBERT M. "The Acquisition of Knowledge." *Psychological Review* 69:355–65 (1962).

———. "The Learning Requirements for Inquiry." *Journal of Research in Science Teaching* 2:144–54 (1964).

———. "Human Problem Solving: Internal and External Events." In *Problem Solving: Research, Method, and Theory,* edited by Benjamin Kleinmuntz, pp. 128–48. New York: Wiley, 1966.

GOODLAD, JOHN I., RENATA VON STOEPHASIUS, and M. FRANCES KLEIN. *The Changing School Curriculum.* New York: The Fund for the Advancement of Education, 1966.

GREENBERG, HERBERT M. *Teaching With Feeling: Compassion and Self-Awareness in the Classroom Today.* New York: Macmillan, 1969.

GUILFORD, J. P. "Intellectual Factors in Productive Thinking." In *Productive Thinking in Education,* edited by Mary Jane Aschner and

Charles E. Bish, pp. 5–20. Washington, D.C.: National Education Association, 1968.

HOLT, JOHN. *How Children Fail.* New York: Pitman, 1964.

HYMAN, RONALD T. *Ways of Teaching.* Philadelphia: Lippincott, 1970.

KORAN, MARY LOU. "The Effects of Individual Differences on Observational Learning in the Acquisition of a Teaching Skill." Paper read at the annual meeting of the American Educational Research Association, Los Angeles, February 1969.

LYND, ALBERT. *Quackery in the Public Schools.* Boston: Little, Brown, 1953.

MAGER, ROBERT F. *Preparing Instructional Objectives.* Palo Alto, California: Fearon, 1962.

MEAD, MARGARET. *Culture and Commitment.* New York: Doubleday, 1970.

PARKER, J. CECIL and LOUIS J. RUBIN. *Process as Content: Curriculum Design and the Application of Knowledge.* Chicago: Rand McNally, 1966.

PARNES, SIDNEY J. "Effects of Extended Effort in Creative Problem Solving." *Journal of Educational Psychology* 52:117–22 (1961).

———— and ARNOLD MEADOW. "Effects of 'Brainstorming' Instructions on Creative Problem Solving by Trained and Untrained Subjects." *Journal of Educational Psychology* 50:171–76 (1959).

PIAGET, JEAN. *The Psychology of Intelligence.* Totowa, N.J.: Littlefield, Adams, 1968.

POSTMAN, NEIL and CHARLES WEINGARTNER. *Teaching as a Subversive Activity.* New York: Delacorte, 1969.

RICKOVER, HYMAN G. *Education and Freedom.* New York: Dutton, 1959.

————. *Swiss Schools and Ours: Why Theirs Are Better.* Boston: Little, Brown, 1962.

————. *American Education, a National Failure: The Problem of Our Schools and What We Can Learn from England.* New York: Dutton, 1963.

ROGERS, CARL R. *Freedom to Learn.* Columbus, Ohio: Charles E. Merrill, 1969.

ROSENTHAL, ROBERT. "Self-Fulfilling Prophecy." *Psychology Today* 2:46–51 (1968).

———— and LENORE JACOBSON. *Pygmalion in the Classroom, Teacher Expectation and Pupils' Intellectual Development.* New York: Holt, Rinehart & Winston, 1968a.

————. "Teacher Expectations for the Disadvantaged." *Scientific American* 218:19–23 (1968b).

SCANDURA, JOSEPH M. "Algorithm Learning and Problem Solving." *The Journal of Experimental Education* 34:1–6 (1966a).

————. "Prior Learning, Presentation Order, and Prerequisite Practice in Problem Solving." *The Journal of Experimental Education* 34:12–18 (1966b).

————. "Problem Solving and Prior Learning." *The Journal of Experimental Education* 34:7–11 (1966c).

———— and MERLYN BEHR. "Prerequisite Practice and Criterion Form in Mathematics Learning." *The Journal of Experimental Education* 35:54–5 (1966).

SCHWAB, JOSEPH J. *College Curriculum and Student Protest.* Chicago: The University of Chicago Press, 1969.

SHERIF, MUZAFER and HADLEY CANTRIL. *The Psychology of Ego-Involvements: Social Attitudes and Identifications.* New York: Wiley, 1947.

SILBERMAN, CHARLES E. *Crisis in the Classroom: The Remaking of American Education.* New York: Random House, 1970.

SMITH, MORTIMER B. *And Madly Teach: A Layman Looks at Public School Education.* Chicago: H. Regnery, 1949.

———. *The Public Schools in Crisis: Some Critical Essays.* Chicago: H. Regnery, 1956.

Index

A

Affect, definition of, 83
Allen, Dwight, 5
Amster, Harriett, 46
Anthropological authority, 86
Aristotle, 24
Authority, types óf, 86-87

B

Bandura, Albert, 8
Behavioral objectives, 17-18
Behr, Merlyn, 46
Bellack, Arno A., 55-56
Benne, Kenneth D., 32, 86
Berlyne, Daniel E., 46
Berman, Louise M., 69
Bestor, Arthur E., 25
Bordin, E. S., 104
Borton, Terry, 27

Brainstorming, 29, 54-55
Bruner, Jerome S., *ix*, 24, 25, 26

C

Cantril, Hadley, 12
Carkhuff, Robert R., 95, 96, 105, 112, 119
Combs, Arthur W., 25, 85
Comments, oral and written, guidelines
    for, 18-19
Concerns, personal, 12
Concerns about teaching, *x*
Concreteness, definition of, 119

D

Davis, O. L., Jr., 7
Dewey, John, 24
Discovery approach, 24
Discovery learning, advantages of, 26